Spiritual
Parenting

DATE DUE	
AUG - 1 1997	

Spiritual
Parenting

A Sourcebook
for Parents and Teachers

Rabbi Steven M. Rosman, Ph.D., M.SC

The Theosophical Publishing House
P.O. Box 270
Wheaton, IL 60189–0270

A publication of the Theosophical Publishing House,
a department of the Theosophical Society in America.

*This publication made possible with
the assistance of the Kern Foundation.*

Library of Congress Cataloging-in-Publication Data

Rosman, Steven M.
    Spiritual parenting : a sourcebook for parents and teachers /
Steven M. Rosman.
      p.   cm.
    "Quest books."
    Includes bibliographical references.
    ISBN 0–8356–0703–8 : $12.00
    1. Religious education of children.   2. Children—Religious life.
3. Spiritual exercises.   I. Title.
BL42.R68   1994
291.4'4—dc20   94–438
                                         CIP

9 8 7 6 5 4 3 2 1 * 94 95 96 97 98 99

I write with a joy for life and a knowledge of love only because such is the quality of my life with my partner, my wife Bari Ziegel, and with our daughter Michal (Mikki) and our son Ilan, who are, without doubt, divine gifts God intended to enter the world via the love Bari and I share.

I love you three very much and thank you for all you do to support me as I do what brings me such fullness of spirit.

Contents

Acknowledgments

have written most of the words on
the pages that follow and borrowed some from others. Thus, while this
book will bear my name, it is the fruit of a harvest that has been graced
by many supportive and talented people who selflessly contributed to its
maturation. It is not unlike a farmer whose harvest depends upon the
quality of seeds, soil, tools, and nurture. My seeds have been given to
me generously by teachers with whom I have been honored to study
or whose wisdom has enriched me through reading. Those whom I
am fortunate to call my teachers include: Deborah Blair, Dr. Gerald
Epstein, Rabbi Joseph Gelberman, Dr. Edward Hoffman, Deanne Mincer,
Professor Peninnah Schram, and Reb Zalman Schachter-Shalomi. And
there are those whose names you will encounter in the pages that follow
who illumine our contemporary world with their insights and some who
continue to illumine our world despite no longer sharing it with us
physically. The seeds of their wisdom are incomparable. I hope that the
fruits of my labor do justice to the quality of their seed-wisdom.

There have been many who have helped me clarify my thoughts and
my language and who have helped prune parts of the text that would have
obscured the wisdom of my teachers. Those who patiently, generously,
and skillfully examined this text include: Dr. Mark Banschick, Andrea

Candee, Dr. Bruce Cooperstein, Barbara Cooperstein, Eve Drogin, Jacque Lima, and Annette Ziemianski.

Observation and copious research have proven beyond challenge that plants shown love and care grow more bountiful than those that suffer a lack of support and attention. Those who have helped shape and nurture the growth of this text include Barbara Hoberman Levine and Aron Hirt-Manheimer.

On a particular occasion, I needed the advice of some storytelling experts. These professionals serve parents daily, week in and week out, on the front lines of their bookstore *Once Upon a Time,* and they guided me to just what I needed when I needed it. These generous professionals are Ann Chase, Jane Gelbard, and Missy Kemper.

Especially, there are those who blessed me with their confidence in my ability to bring valuable seeds to fruition, with their expert pruning, their nourishment of my ideas and vision, and with their constant nurture of the fruit and its farmer. These people include: Brenda Rosen and John White.

I would also like to thank all of the following for their permission to use or adapt some of the exercises found in this book:

Dawn Publications, 14618 Tyler Foote Road, Nevada City, CA 95959, 916–292–3484, for their permission to adapt "Tree Imagery" and "Camera" from *Sharing The Joy of Nature* by Joseph Cornell (1989).

DeVorss & Company, Box 550, Marina del Rey, CA 90204 and the author Barbara Milicevic for their permissions to use the following yoga exercises from *Your Spiritual Child* by Barbara Milicevic (1984): "Arms Up," "Bottoms Up," "Triangle Pose," "Neck Rolls," pp. 63, 64, 67, and "Rag Doll Bend," "Side Bends," "Cow-Cat Pose," and "Cobra Pose," pp. 71, 74.

Dr. Gerald Epstein for permission to use his exercise "The Garden Of Eden" found in his book *Healing Visualizations: Creating Health Through Imagery,* pp. 198–99, New York: Bantam, 1989. Dr. Epstein credits his teacher Mme. Colette Aboulker-Muscat with being the author of this exercise.

Planetary Publications, P.O. Box 66, 14700 West Park Ave., Boulder Creek, CA 95006 and Deborah Rozman, Ph.D. for permission to use or adapt the following meditations from the book *Meditation for Children* by Deborah Rozman, Ph.D. (2nd edition, 1989): "A Meditation for Three- to Five-Year-Olds," pp. 64–65; "A Meditation for Six- to Ten-Year-Olds," pp. 70–71; and "The Five Senses Meditation," p. 108.

Sri Rama Publishing, Box 2550, Santa Cruz, CA 95603 for permission to use the following asanas from *A Child's Garden of Yoga* by Baba Hari Dass (1980): "Deep Breathing Exercises," "Palm Tree," "Flat on the Floor," "Bow," "Thunderbolt," "Rest Pose," "Salute to the Sun," and "Tree Pose."

Don G. Campbell for permission to use the lists of musical recommendations from the section entitled "Choosing Music for Use in Imagery and Healing" from his book *Music: Physician for Times to Come,* pp. 252–53, published by Quest Books, Wheaton, IL 1991.

Before you read further, imagine . . .

Imagine that your children

Your grandchildren

Your students

Are sitting before you:

There on the floor around you

or in your lap.

What do you want to give them in the time you will share?

Who do you want to help them become?

Who do you want to be for them?

What impressions will your moments in their lives leave on their hearts and souls?

Preface

A few years ago while lecturing in Costa Rica, I conducted a workshop with five- and six-year-old Jewish children in which I used a guided imaginal journey to explore their notions of God and prayer. It was the first time any of the children had used their imaginations in this way. In just a few minutes they became relaxed as we imagined shrinking so small that we could actually climb aboard words of prayer and ride them on a mystical journey through the cosmos. Although they may not have not taken a journey on the wings of prayer before, these children, like children everywhere, take imaginal journeys all the time; they just don't label what it is they have done or where they have gone.

The discussion that followed was as spirited as you might imagine. The children were eager to describe their journeys. Some were so enthusiastic that they could not wait to be called on and simply blurted out descriptions of outer space, of the cloud-filled heavens, and of secret places only God and children know about. Later, while I was conducting a program for a group of women in the community, the mother of one of the children told me that her son had come home from his session with me all excited and had rushed to guide her through the same imaginal journey. Such enthusiasm is not uncommon, for children are inherently energized by the spiritual dimension of life whether encountered on imaginal journeys, on a backyard hike, or in the inner realms of meditation.

Pollsters, sociologists, and trendwatchers tell us that we live in a time when more and more Americans profess belief in God or some positive ineffable spiritual force, and those same polls report that many of our neighbors, co-workers, best friends, and spouses have turned to yoga, meditation, and other spiritual disciplines to create a link between their everyday lives and the transcendent. Despite the escalating desire of increasing numbers of Americans to experience spirituality in their lives, most of us complain that we have little discretionary time and income to devote to such a transforming pursuit. So, what can we do?

My experience in Costa Rica, as well as elsewhere, has shown me that spiritual exercises like imaginal journeys and meditation can satisfy the appetite for transformation expressed by so many today. Sharing such exercises also might be a wonderful way to strengthen family relationships, and it is encouraging to know that spiritual exercises can be done conveniently at home in a surprisingly little amount of time and at little cost. My wife works during the week, and I often work weekends. Yet we have found ways to make spiritual exercises part of our lives. Living a busy lifestyle and conducting workshops for more than ten years for busy parents all over the world enables me to say with confidence that all parents can find the path that is right and comfortable for them and their children.

This book is a beginner's sourcebook for exercises and activities that parents, grandparents, teachers, clergy, and others working with children can use to help themselves and their children grow spiritually. While the emphasis in my title is on children, clearly they do not live in a vacuum. To the extent that we can make these same practices and attitudes part of our daily lives, our children will be encouraged to do the same. After all, we are our children's first and most important teachers.

The Introduction talks about how we can help nourish the innate spirituality of our children. It explains the basic terms you will come upon as you read this book, and it discusses why I believe these exercises and tools are beneficial and will work for you. Also, the introductory material furnishes some general guidelines for how to use the book, how to approach guiding children of different ages through the exercises, and how to adapt the exercises to individual needs and styles.

Part One contains a selection of preparatory exercises that will help children and their adult guides relax and promote awareness of bodily sensations and rhythms. It offers suggestions about how to get started and about how to use music, storytelling, breathing exercises, purification rituals, yoga, and meditation as means of nurturing the innate spiritual capacities of your children and as ways to prepare them for the exercises that come in the last two sections. Finally, it addresses how we adults might find ways to bring spirituality into our lives and our children's lives despite the many legitimate obligations and concerns with which we must cope day in and day out.

Parts Two and Three present spiritual exercises under the rubrics of "Going Outside" and "Going Inside." I have chosen to include nine exercises in each of these two sections. In the ancient world, nine was the all-powerful 3 x 3, the numbers of completion, synthesis, and fulfillment. The ancient sages considered three the perfect number as it represented beginning, middle, and end. So, 3 x 3 was considered a most perfect and powerful spiritual multiplication. Since nine appears prominently in this basic ancient notion (as well as in Christian symbolism as the three triple triads of choirs of angels, in Graeco-Roman symbolism as the nine gods and nine muses, in Kabbalistic teaching representing the *sefirra* or ninth divine emanation known as Foundation, in Hindu tradition as the square of nine forming the mandala of eighty-one squares that leads to and encloses the universe, and in Buddhist tradition as the supreme spiritual power), it seemed particularly appropriate to structure the number of exercises accordingly.

"Going Outside" focuses on exercises like naturewalks, trail hikes, scavenger hunts, meditations, and imaginal journeys that use the flora and fauna of the natural world as spiritual foci allowing our children to get out into the world, to run around, and to sense the marvels that surround them daily. "Going Inside" offers exercises with internal foci to help them turn inward. Each of these exercises is presented with a consistent format, a recommended script, and directions. Whenever a particular type of exercise is presented for the first time, there are prefatory remarks that furnish recommendations about settings, postures, and practices that might prove helpful to beginners.

Finally, there is information for those who wish to go further. The book concludes with a bibliography and an extensive list of resources that, over the years, have proven helpful to me and other seekers of the spiritual dimension of living.

I, myself, am a parent and a teacher. So I wish to all of you who seek to guide your children or your students a fruitful start on a lifelong path of shared discovery and wonder. Abraham Joshua Heschel, rabbi and philosopher, once taught that those who sense the wonder, share the wonder. Children have a natural openness to the world of outer and inner experience that is unobstructed by logic and too much thinking. They are refreshing and they refresh us. These next pages give us a chance to allow our children to reawaken us to sunsets and butterflies, to watching bubbles float upon the breeze, and to trying to catch fireflies in our hands.

An old Buddhist tale tells us of a time that the Buddha was stopped by a man on the road. This man was absolutely taken with the illumined presence of the Buddha and asked him if he had become so radiant through any extraordinary means.

"No," replied the Buddha with characteristic gentleness and patience.

"Then you must be some sort of sorcerer whose magic has transformed you into an enlightened being."

Again, the Buddha looked at the man kindly and told him that there was, indeed, nothing extraordinary about him, except...

"Except what?" pleaded the man.

"Except I am awake," replied the Buddha.

And if you have ever tried to sleep late on a day off, you know that it is a penchant of children to awaken their parents.

That is among their many gifts to us.

Introduction:
Sense the Wonder

"Education is not to fill a bucket, it is to kindle a fire."

Herodotus

"Education of children should be considered from five points of view: physical, mental, moral, social, and spiritual."

Hazrat Inayat Khan

"The world was not created for us to enjoy, but we are created in order to evolve the cosmos."

Maria Montessori

"They who sense the wonder share in the wonder."

Abraham Joshua Heschel

My daughter Michal (Mikki) was born in Danbury Hospital, in Danbury, Connecticut, on April 3, 1989. For months leading up to her birth, my greatest fear was not whether I would faint or whether we would forget our Lamaze bag of snacks and sundry items. I was panicked that I would not be able to cry when our child, born of the love I share with my life-partner Bari, was brought into this world in which we live.

As a man-in-training, I had been instructed not to cry. Men do not cry. So, being a good student who wanted to be a good man, I learned not to cry. No matter how many times I read *Love Story* or saw the film *It's A Wonderful Life*, I could not cry. A lump always formed in my throat large enough to gag me, but I was not liberated enough to shatter the invisible membrane separating me from my True Self and bring on the gift of tears.

In the operating room prior to the C-Section, everything happened so fast. Although usually squeamish at the sight of blood—I used to close my eyes when Popeye and Bluto fought—the frenetic pace of procedures and the flow of my adrenalin kept me standing and coherent. Before I knew it, Mikki emerged from an incision made at about the same place the Japanese call the *hara*. From that classical source of life energy or *ki*, our child was born. And I sobbed. Tears cascaded down my cheeks and bathed my trembling lips with their warm salt water. I felt cleansed and whole as I had never felt before.

From the moment children are born, they hold the potential to renew in us adults an inherent spirituality and connection to the wellsprings of life itself that we have become too busy, too occupied, too educated, and too narrowly focused to experience very often, if at all.

As Mikki has grown through these first four years of her life, my friends have noticed as many changes in me as developmental transformations in her. Consequently, some of my friends call Mikki my "little Buddha." How true! And like Mikki, your children can help you find the enlightenment that each day with them can bring. Beauty no longer has to be complex, or thematically consistent. Discovery does not have to happen according to specific rules. Play does not have to be for winning. Love does not always have to be explained. There have been moments when Mikki and I have watched clouds together while reclining on the top of a grassy knoll. There have been spontaneous cries of glee from both of us when we have found a butterfly or a robin's nest. We talk about our dreams and do yoga together in the early morning sunrise. We simply say, "Wow!" when the sun sets and take turns identifying the colors of the metamorphosing sky as day gives way to night. At bedtime, we sense the calming rhythms of evening as we lie down together, Mikki with her stuffed animals and me watching her, holding her hand and marveling at the miracle Bari, I, and the Universe brought into this world. Gentle music, whose tone and timbre, meter and melody echo our heartbeats and reflect the states of our souls, envelopes us. Story time grants us an opportunity to step through the porous membrane that separates waking world from imaginal world. Linear logic no longer dominates our lives in the imaginal realm, neither does time or space. Together Mikki and I walk the landscape of mystery where everything is possible, and all is filled with wonder. Every people has known at some time in its past the spiritual power of stories. Each night, Mikki and I reclaim that legacy and experience its numinosity.

Conversations with my friends tell me that no matter how unique my relationship is with Mikki, they have tales to tell as well. For instance, my friend Marty has two sons, Marc and Eric. Marc is about four at this moment. Marty recently told me that this past July, Marc saw his first fireworks display. Sliding into his sleeping bag a few hours later, he asked his daddy, "Who do the fireworks help?"

Tough question, right? It is amazing how kids can humble you with just one question. So Marty, being the bright physician that he is, took Marc's question to mean that he understood that everything—even fireworks—has a purpose. Armed with his years of medical training and practical pediatric clinical practice, Marty explained that fireworks exist to make you feel special and wonderful.

Marc considered his father's wisdom and asked, "You mean God was there?"

Marty told me he prays that he might be blessed to see things as clearly as his four-year-old son more often.

If nothing else, the exercises in this book will afford you and your children precious time to spend together so their inherent spiritual clarity might rub off just a bit.

BUT SOMETIMES LIFE HAPPENS

Despite our best intentions, life happens. Obligations arise, crises strike, snafus occur, car-pools become disrupted. Some things never seem to change. Listen to the words of Anne Morrow Lindbergh, written almost forty years ago:

> I mean to lead a simple life . . . But I do not. I find that my frame does not foster simplicity. My husband and five children must make their way in the world. The life I have chosen as wife and mother entrains a whole caravan of complications. It involves a house in the suburbs and either household drudgery or household help which wavers between scarcity and non-existence for most of us. It involves food and shelter; meals, planning, marketing, bills, and making the ends meet in a thousand ways. It involves not only the butcher, the baker, the candlestickmaker but countless other experts to keep my modern house with its modern "simplifications" (electricity, plumbing, refrigerator, gas-stove, oil-burner, dish-washer, radios, car, and numerous other labor-saving devices) functioning properly. It involves health; doctors, dentists, appointments, medicine, cod-liver oil, vitamins, trips to the drugstore. It involves education, spiritual, intellectual, physical; schools, school conferences, car-pools, extra trips for basket-ball or orchestra practice; tutoring; camps, camp equip-ment and transportation. It involves clothes, shopping, laundry, cleaning, mending, letting skirts down and sewing buttons on, or finding someone else to do it. It involves friends, my hus-band's, my children's, my own, and endless arrangements to get together; letters, invitations, telephone calls and transportation hither and yon.
>
> For life today in America is based on the premise of ever-widening circles of contact and communication. It involves not only family demands, but community demands, national de-mands, international demands on the good citizen, through social and cultural pressures, through newspapers, magazines, radio programs, political drives, charitable appeals, and so on. My mind reels with it . . . This is not the life of simplicity but the life of multiplicity that the wise men warn us of. It leads not to unification but to fragmentation. It does not bring grace; it destroys the soul . . . The problem is . . . how to remain whole in the midst of the distractions of life; how to remain balanced, no

matter what centrifugal forces tend to pull one off center; how to remain strong, no matter what shocks come in at the periphery and tend to crack the hub of the wheel.[1]

Sociologists, psychologists, and philosophers have observed that today, like yesteryear, we are often overstimulated, overworked, overwhelmed, and overstressed. We are sometimes underappreciated, underloved, and underdeveloped. The stress of contemporary life poses threats to our health and well-being, as it does for our children, too.

Having it all, expecting to have it all, and being expected to learn it all at earlier and earlier ages have consumed some of our children in a bonfire of our vanities. Psychologist David Elkind of Tufts University has called this latest generation of children "hurried children."[2] Some of our children are pressured to hurry and grow up, to achieve, to succeed, and to please. Yardsticks seem to be everywhere in their lives; not, however, to measure the inches they have grown since their last birthdays, but rather to evaluate the extent to which they have "measured up" to the adult standards of achievement that are often deleterious to these children's health and childhoods. According to Elkind, hurried children often fail at school, abuse drugs, complain chronically of psychosomatic ailments, appear to be unhappy, and seem lethargic.[3] Childhood once had a life span of at least a dozen years; now for so many that has been tragically curtailed by as much as half. In her own work with children around the country, educator and therapist Maureen Murdock has found that our children are, indeed, hurried children overwhelmed by the demands of their lifestyles. She vividly recalls an instance when a group of third-graders complained to her that they hate rushing from school to soccer practice. They want time just to sit and be children. They feel rushed and stressed by overbearing, precision schedules. The one symbol that appeared most in the drawings they did with Murdock was—a ticking alarm clock![4]

The alarm may have sounded just in time. Our children are manifesting the unhealthy symptoms and maladies of contemporary life; they can also lead us back to simpler, healthier, more integrated and spiritual lifestyles. Some things *can* change.

Imagine, for a moment, that our lives and our children's lives are represented by a big bowl of water. Inside the bowl are several glittering, precious stones. Imagine their brilliance. If you place your hand in the water and begin to churn it, the motion of the water begins to distort the appearance of the stones. If you churn fast enough, the turbulence will obscure the stones altogether.[5] But if you still the waters and look inside, you and your children may begin to realize your spiritual birthrights and the divinity that inheres within us all. Some have called that way of being *mindfulness*, while others call it *yishuv ha'da-at* (settling the mind). No matter what people call it, its characteristics are similar: a stilling of the mind, a calming of the spirit, a focus on our inner wisdom, a centeredness, a stability, a quiet strength. While it cannot be bought, it can be developed—through spiritual exercise.

WHAT ARE SPIRITUAL EXERCISES?

To begin, let me clarify what I mean by the term *spiritual*. It seems to appear everywhere in this new age of ours, yet it is rarely defined. So I offer several definitions for the term as I use it in the course of this book.

First and foremost, *spirituality* refers to an intense, personal, awe-based concern for questions about life and meaning, as opposed to *religion,* a traditional collection of institutionalized and canonized doctrines, rituals, rites, and creeds about those same questions. I believe that religion is born out of spiritual experience. It is the "Amen" punctuating a spontaneous prayer uttered in the midst of an ineffable experience of awesome wonder. Historically, it seems as though religious people worshiped their answers and forfeited an openness to the kind of direct experience of the Awesome, the No-thing, the Unity of Unities that originally inspired their saints and prophets. Children's spirituality is evidenced by their curiosity, their penchant for asking questions about where this comes from or why that is the way it is, and their innocent appreciation of the world around them that some might call worshipful.

Second, anthropologist Ashley Montagu defines *spiritual* as "that combination of qualities that make up the person's attitudes of mind toward himself and to the world about him. . . . It is the need to love others and to be loved; the qualities of curiosity, inquisitiveness, thirst for knowledge; the need to learn; imagination; creativity, openmindedness, experimental-mindedness; the sense of humor, playfulness, joy; the optimism, honesty, resilience, and compassionate intelligence—that constitute the spirit of the child."[6]

Third, Rabbi Arthur Green, author and respected teacher, believes that *spiritual* is "life in the presence of God."[7] By this definition, children's spirituality might appear as their awe when confronted by the transcendent mysteries of the universe.

I define *spiritual exercises* as those vehicles that enable our children to still the waters of their lives long enough to perceive how precious they are, awaken them to the majesty of life in all its mystery, help them to intuit the unity of all things, make them aware of the power of love and of loving, encourage their imagination, impel their curiosity, inspire a sense of humor, playfulness, and compassion, evoke wonder, inspire questions without concern for answers, and strengthen self-esteem and self-reliance.

Not every spiritual exercise in this book will be comfortable or preferable for every child. Classical Hindu masters taught that there were several kinds of yoga because there were several types of people. Such is the case regarding spiritual exercises and our children. Some children delight in the outdoors. Some love to dwell in their imaginations. Some express themselves through physical movement. Others respond best to visual or auditory cues. Jewish tradition teaches that although the Creator used the same press to make each human being, we each emerged unique. I have endeavored to provide variety and opportunities for you to make gross or subtle adjustments to the exercises so that your children can find themselves mirrored and honored.

NOT ONLY IN A MONASTERY

There are many who believe or who teach, mistakenly, that spirituality can be pursued only in the isolated settings of monasteries and ashrams. This approach to spirituality appears to be based upon the conviction that there is a clear and irreconcilable distinction between spirituality and worldliness, as if one who lives in the world of community and mundanity cannot find the path to the spiritual dimension of existence. I believe this is not true, and many great spiritual teachers in this century like Martin Buber, Abraham Joshua Heschel, G.I. Gurdjieff, Thich Nhat Hanh, Eugene Kennedy, Pir Vilayat Inayat Khan, Zalman Schachter-Shalomi, and Chögyam Trungpa, help us find just such a path of this world and in this world.

Children themselves are the greatest refutation of that "monastery" argument. Children are undeniably and profoundly worldly and spiritual at the same time. Many years ago I was working at a camp and happened to be on a hike with six- and seven-year-olds. For the "expert" of the group, I was not much help for some aspects of our exploration. Raised in the Bronx, I did not know much about poison ivy or poison oak. Bees I knew about; we had them even in the Bronx. There was one child, Peter, who had been raised in a more rural environment than I had been raised in. (I guess it would not be so hard to find someone who knew more about poison ivy than I. I hear that they even had parks and gardens in Brooklyn!) He led the way and I followed; that was as it should be. As the day grew late, the sun began to set. There we were, six campers and a hapless adult "guide," but what a glorious sunset it was! Peter and a friend were running amidst the rocks and challenging one another to see who could be the first to hit a tree across the way with a stone. Suddenly, they stopped—as if they had been paralyzed by a martian ray gun. They were enthralled by the sunset, and I overheard Peter tell his friend, in a very matter of fact tone that it was a good day for God, too: Because God was in such a good mood, S/He decided to paint the sky to show S/He was happy.

Peter and other children whom I have met during my workshops have taught me that one can be very spiritual while living the routine daily life of a suburban, urban, or rural child. It is true for us, too—we parents and teachers who will guide our children though these exercises. Life does happen, and some days do get mangled in red tape. Yet the Hindus taught that there were a couple of paths to spiritual initiation: one was through the monastery, and one was through parenting.[8] Even the great gurus agreed that one could walk the path to spiritual illumination as a parent, despite the attendant rigors of family life. The path of family does present some obstacles not found in the serene, isolated life of a monastery though: hurdling piles of laundry, racing to car-pools, juggling meals and dishes, supervising homework, tending to skinned knees, and comforting tears of fright, frustration, or disappointment.

I suppose that those wise Hindu masters knew that both spiritual paths had their advantages. Those of us blessed by children and students gain from spending time with our own younger walking, talking apprehenders of the awesome, the sublime, and the sacred. Like diviners, they hone right in on the very core of illumination, and we are lucky enough to have them around to help us.

Consequently, rather than separating the teachings and exercises in this book from the flow of your children's routine daily activities, try to integrate them and the awareness they engender into ordinary living time. One day at a time. One hour at a time. One moment at a time. There will be days when this is more difficult than others. But, hey, life happens. Use this book selectively, and you will find that you and your children will discover your own paths to your mutual and individual delight.

The Buddhist teacher Jack Kornfield has reminded us: "Parenting is a labor of love. It's a path of service and surrender and, like the practice of a Buddha or bodhisattva (a seeker of enlightenment), it demands patience, understanding and tremendous sacrifice. It is also a way to reconnect with the mystery of life."9

9

THE TIME IS RIGHT

Twentieth-century psychology has described children variously according to developmental schemes, or as psychodynamic cauldrons of predominantly id-like energy, or as creatures who are driven by habit and shaped in response to the external stimuli they encounter, but not generally as spiritual beings. That is, until recently.

In his groundbreaking book *Visions of Innocence*, psychologist Edward Hoffman argues that children indeed are spiritual beings who have peak spiritual experiences. Yet because they lack the language to articulate ineffable experiences of the Infinite, we adults might ignore, deride, or at best, fail to recognize their inherent spiritual capacities. Contemporary psychology's myopia, however, is countered by the historical wisdom of the world's spiritual traditions. For example, Jewish mystics taught centuries ago that we are exposed to the deepest secrets of the universe during our fetal existence and are made to forget upon birth.[10] In a different land hundreds of years earlier, Jesus recognized the innate spiritual capacity of children and defended their presence among his audiences. It is said that on at least one occasion he cautioned unenlightened adults not to hinder the children among them, "for to such belong the kingdom of heaven. Truly I say to you: whoever does not receive the Kingdom of God like a child shall not enter it."[11]

The time has come to reclaim such traditional wisdom and make our children the beneficiaries. Children are magical beings born with a wisdom that their eyes convey to us even when they are newly born. Just the smell of our own infants, the touch of their little hands, and the beat of their hearts regulating our own heal us and place our priorities in perspective pretty quickly.

Until quite recently, intelligence was defined narrowly and tested for accordingly. Aside from the cultural and sexist biases that were part of the test designs, children comparatively less verbal and mathematical-logical than others did not test as well as their peers. They were punished by lower achievement scores and fewer opportunities for entrance into elite academic programs that also focused upon logical-verbal intelligence. Then along came researchers like Howard Gardner of Harvard University whose studies, contained in his book *Frames of Mind: The Theory of Multiple Intelligences*, exploded the myths surrounding intelligence testing and defining. Consequently, the notion of a single intelligence that can be measured by a specific test has been challenged articulately and convincingly. Gardner argues that rather than a single intelligence, we are born with the potential to develop a multiplicity of intelligences—for example, the potential for musical accomplishment, for spatial reasoning, for bodily kinesthetic mastery, and others. Gardner calls for an expansion of the conventional view of intelligence to include these multiple forms previously overlooked by society and especially by our testing professionals.

I am grateful for Gardner's work because, in broadening our understanding of intelligences, he makes it possible to suggest that if he identifies at least seven intelligences *in potentia*, there may someday be consensus agreement about an eighth or a ninth kind. Someday, I believe that researchers like Gardner are going to "discover" an intelligence of the heart.

Long ago, King Solomon valued this intelligence of the heart more than any other imaginable gift. Jewish tradition teaches that when he had finished the construction of the Temple in Jerusalem, God offered him any reward he would name. Solomon asked for *lev shamaya*, the wisdom of the heart. According to these traditions, it would seem to me that Solomon's intelligence was a heartfelt, intuitive, spiritual intelligence. Children are born with it. Adults, if they are fortunate, rediscover it.

In his book *Waking Dream Therapy*, Gerald Epstein points out that the part of the brain mediating functions like the imagination is the right hemisphere, and I believe that it is no coincidence that this hemisphere of the brain is connected with the functions on the left side of the body where the heart is located. Ancient traditions like the Jewish tradition, the ancient Egyptian tradition, and the Native American tradition call this right brain/imaginal/heart connection the intelligence of the heart. Such intelligence was the cornerstone of spirituality in the ancient world; it is the natural spirituality of our children, and through our children, it can be ours again, too.

I am convinced that the works of Abraham Maslow,[12] Roberto Assagioli,[13] Edward Hoffman, and others suggest that this intelligence of the heart, like all of the varied kinds of intelligences, inheres within the souls of our children as potential. And like those other types of intelligences, spirituality exists as potential until it is catalyzed. The spiritual exercises included in this book are among the best ways to catalyze that vital potential.

The time is right. The time is now.

WHAT CAN YOU EXPECT FROM READING THIS BOOK?

In the course of reading this book, you will discover resources that will help you and your children simplify, unify, and enrich your lives—not from outside, but from within. You need not have had any prior encounter with the ancient and modern wisdom that I will share with you. You need not have any particular religious conviction. The exercises contained in this book are clearly and fully described. They are adaptable to the particularities of any religious tradition and to the lifestyles and the needs of any family and any professionals who work with children.

Part One of the text is called "Getting Ready." There you will find tips for preparing yourself to conduct a session of spiritual exercises and for creating a physical and emotional environment conducive to the experience. You will also be introduced to meditation, basic yoga postures, breathing exercises, the art of storytelling, purification rituals, and relaxation techniques that will help you and your children get your physical selves and your inner, spiritual selves ready for the exercises to come. Don't worry! Every term will be defined and every ritual and exercise will be described and explained fully. My working presumption is that you have little or no experience with exercises like these. Here is a place for you to begin.

In Part Two, entitled "Going Outside," you will discover many ways to help your children and yourselves grow spiritually through contact with the wonder-filled world of nature. The eighteenth-century Chasidic rebbe Nahum of Tchernobil taught us that we can find God's presence everywhere. "There is nothing," he said, "besides the presence of God . . . and the presence of the Creator remains in each created thing." So it would seem that in walking amidst the flora and fauna of our world, we might come into "the presence of God" at any given moment.

In Part Three, entitled "Going Inside," we will explore our inner selves. The greatest classic of Jewish mystical literature, the *Zohar*, taught us that we human beings are a microcosm of the universe. Just as a cell reveals the secrets and wonders of the body, so the inner landscape of the person reveals the secrets and wonders of the universe. The exercises in this section furnish the tools that help us quiet the turbulence swirling around us so we might explore the wisdom residing in our innermost beings.

I based my selection of these exercises on my experience with children around the world, on the guidance of modern psychologists, on the advice of holistic educators, on my understanding of the wisdom of the world's great religious traditions and spiritual masters, and on the lessons of my own spiritual teachers whose names you will encounter as you read. I consider all of these classical and contemporary sages to be my teachers.

Wherever possible, I have let them speak to you in their own words and instruct you in their own exercises.

In introducing each exercise, I will discuss its background and define any unfamiliar terms. I will also let you know what you need to have on hand to do the exercise, and, if necessary, I will provide some recommendations to help children with specific needs to enjoy this exercise in their own special ways. However, because all children are unique, please feel free to emend and augment any of my exercises as needed.

At times there will be a script prepared for you to use that is the essence of that exercise. When any script is provided, please read through it carefully to familiarize yourself with it. Feel free to adapt it for the special needs of your children as you see fit. None of the scripts or directions is gospel. You know your children best. My experience conducting workshops for children of various ages around the world helps me give you some options you might find valuable. If not, invent your own remedies, alter the directions and scripts to better reflect your style, your experience, and the needs of your children. In some cases, the exercises will not be based upon a script, but rather upon some directions. Please feel free to adapt and emend here as I suggested you might do with regard to the scripted exercises.

NOTES

1. Anne Morrow Lindbergh, *Gift from the Sea* (New York: Vintage Books, 1991), pp. 25 27, 29.

2. David Elkind, *The Hurried Child: Growing Up Too Fast Too Soon* (Reading, MA: Addison-Wesley Publishing Company, 1981), p. xii.

3. Elkind, p. xii.

4. Maureen Murdock, *Spinning Inward: Using Guided Imagery with Children for Learning, Creativity, & Relaxation* (Boston: Shambhala Publications, 1987), p. 17.

5. This imagery is adapted from Karey Solomon's essay "The Blossoming Soul," in *Spiritual Parenting in the New Age*, ed. Anne Carson (Freedom, CA: The Crossing Press, 1989), p. 126.

6. Ashley Montagu, *Growing Young* (New York: McGraw-Hill Book Company, 1981), p. 117.

7. Arthur Green, ed. *Jewish Spirituality: From the Bible Through the Middle Ages* (New York: The Crossroad Publishing Company, 1986), p. xiii.

8. Della Belansky, "Parenthood as Spiritual Training," in *A Theosophical Guide for Parents* (Ojai, CA: Parents Theosophical Research Group, 1981), p. 25.

9. Jack Kornfield, "A Parent's Guide to Conscious Childraising: Conscious Parenting," *Common Boundary* 2 (January/February 1993): 24.

10. Edward Hoffman, *Visions of Innocence: Spiritual and Inspirational Experiences of Childhood* (Boston: Shambhala Publications, 1992), p. 3.

11. Hoffman, p. 3.

12. Abraham Maslow (1908–1970) was best known as a personality theorist who was interested in motivational structure. In his work as a psychologist, he emphasized the inherent goodness in human beings. He postulated a hierarchical model of human motivation that ascended from basic biological needs to those of self-actualization. Maslow believed that the fundamental nature of the individual is essentially spiritual.

13. Roberto Assagioli (1888–1974) was among the pioneers of psychoanalysis in Italy and a colleague of Freud and Jung. He evolved a comprehensive psychology that he called Psychosynthesis. Assagioli believed that Psychosynthesis brought together personality and spirituality, and he sought to merge the scientific elements of psychology with elements of mysticism to create an integrated understanding of human nature.

14

Part One

Getting
Ready

Finding the Right Time and Place

We are creatures of habit, and our children are no different. We all get out of bed on the same side every morning. After that, we wash, brush our teeth, get dressed, and put each piece of clothing on in the same order as we did the day before. We usually eat the same food every morning, and so do our children—if we can get them to eat at all. Our children sit in the same seats on the same school buses just as we sit in the same seats on the same trains. There is a routine to our children's daily activities, and usually the same pertains to the evening. We join our children watching the same television shows at the same times each night. We turn off the television and follow the same routines in preparing for bed each night.

Habits can be positive or negative, depending on what behavior, attitude, or activity we reinforce constantly. When our children become habituated to a routine, to particular reading or viewing material, or even to listening to specific radio stations, they internalize a way of life and a way of looking at our world.

Spiritual exercises spawn habits that help nurture a spiritual way of looking at the world. In a few minutes each day as a family or as a class, we can explore the mysteries of our existence and the wonder of being alive. This book will help you make spiritual exercises a daily ritual for your children, your students, and yourselves.

To facilitate the development of a ritual, choose a specific time (there are many who suggest twilight or before bedtime), place in the home or school, and day(s) of the week. Unplug the telephone and eliminate any other predictable distractions. Invite your children to help decorate your sacred space with those ceremonial, traditional, and ancestral objects that create the atmosphere you all want. Together you might select certain mats or rugs, tapestries or wall hangings, heirlooms or ritual objects, family pictures or paintings, inspirational signs or favorite prayers. Together you might find a specific kind of incense or fragrance. It may take a while for your children to grow accustomed to incense or diffused essential oils. Be patient with them: introduce them to one incense or oil on one day, and when they seem ready, try a different one on another day. Spend some time with your children considering the kind of lighting you want or whether you wish to be near windows. Explore different ways of calling your children to the spiritual exercise sessions. Some may prefer a bell, and others might prefer the sound of music. There may even be those who like to join in the recitation of a prayer as a kind of "call to worship," or to sing a song as they enter the sacred space that they have created with you. Consider asking all who enter this sacred space to remove their shoes, wear some type of ritual head-covering, or don a particular kind of ritual garment in order to contribute to the exclusive and consecrated nature of this special place. My recommendation is that you make your decisions and keep them as constant as possible. After a while, you may discover that merely the sound of a certain instrument, the whiff of a fragrance, the sight of an image, the sound of the first notes of a song, or the step into a room evoke very specific spiritual responses in your children.

WHAT ABOUT MY BUSY SCHEDULE ?

Who is not busy these days? Those with careers outside of the home need to balance working schedules with school or day care schedules, children's car-pools with train and travel schedules, office work done at home with family "quality time" schedules. Those who care for the home and family full time need to balance shopping schedules with play group schedules, home maintenance schedules with piano lessons and basketball practices, meal coordination with individual family members' arrival and departure schedules.

Don't set yourself up for failure. Don't commit to three or four days a week of spiritual exercises if that is not possible right away. Don't commit to a fixed time on the clock if each day's schedule is unpredictable. Sure, it may be great if you can devote four or five days a week to these exercises and establish a fixed time and place for them, but do not stop breathing just because you cannot make each breath a long, relaxed, full one! Any long, relaxed, full breath you can bring into your body provides more oxygen for your cells and drives more stress from your life than if you never decided to breathe that way. Eventually, the pleasure of a long, relaxed, full breath impels you to experience it more often. You find you really miss those breaths when you cannot take them. Take one now. Don't worry about style or doing it "right"—just do it. Breathe in through your nose as slowly as you can. Hold the breath at the end of your inhalation for a few seconds. Feel the pleasure of fully inflated lungs and the power and energy inside you. Then exhale slowly. Feel your body relax. Feel it detoxify from stress. The pleasures and sensations of long, full breathing can be intoxicating. They are their own motivation.

Try to read this book from cover to cover. Try to include these exercises in the lives of your children as often as possible. Please do not judge yourself harshly if circumstances occasionally arise that prevent you from spending this time with your children. It seems to me that such judgment would contradict the intelligence of the heart that is the core of our own and our children's spirituality. Try to find time for a short exercise if you do not have time for a long one. In some cases it may be best to exercise with one child in the afternoon and another in the evening.

I believe with all my heart and soul that if you make these exercises a part of your children's lives and your own, whenever and however you can, you will notice the changes they bring to your life and the lives of your children, and will find that you always have enough time to exercise spiritually. Those beginning this path will join the tens of thousands and more for whom spiritual exercises have become an intoxicating and detoxifying elixir—the energy and essence of life.

HOW DO I BEGIN?

These suggestions are for parents, grandparents, teachers, and clergy:

1. Become comfortable and familiar with the exercises. There is no doubt that you are your children's role model. You are their teachers and their spiritual guides. Children learn by imitation and identification. They will apprehend your joy and delight or your discomfort and displeasure. Those kinds of nonverbal signals are as significant for your children's own spiritual growth as actually doing any of the exercises.

2. If you are conducting an exercise for yourself and others, I recommend that you first read through the exercise you wish to lead many times. It seems most natural if you can lead without referring to a written text. Because it is so important, I wish to reiterate here that there is no need to adhere to the instructions in this book word for word. Feel free to phrase the instructions in your own way. Add your own touches and make the exercises yours. Speak slowly and confidently, trying to express love, acceptance, and enthusiasm with your voice. Become comfortable with silence. Allow for pauses as indicated by the ellipses (. . .) in the text.

3. Try to anticipate and plan for difficulties or obstacles that might arise as you lead your children through the exercises. Along the way I have offered recommendations for just such occasions. Use them as you would advice from a friend. You are the expert on your children. Trust yourself, as they do. Experiment, and send your success stories to me.

4. In general, please do not judge yourself or your children. You may feel awkward and unsure at the beginning. Acceptance of such feelings is an important first step on the path of spiritual growth. These exercises are not competitions or trials. "Correct" and "incorrect" are irrelevant and harmful evaluations that ought not to be a part of your vocabulary when engaging in these exercises. They are loving and delicious experiences to be shared by all.

5. Children need trustworthy and secure environments. They may feel uncomfortable at first or even for some time with the exercises. Young

children may not want to close their eyes when such a response is ordinarily called for. That is okay. If your children are reluctant to participate, you might simply allow them to observe. In their own time, after seeing you enjoying these exercises regularly, they may express interest. Please do not compel them to join in or coax them too much. Respect their reluctance, honor their individual talents and frustrations, but also show them that you approach these exercises in a respectful and enthusiastic way. (Incidentally, the word *enthusiasm* is a most appropriate word in this case. It comes from the Greek *en* plus *theos*, meaning "in God," "in spirit," or "inspired.")

6. The "imaginal muscle" does not get much exercise in our daily lives. It may be that the imaginal journeys presented in this book will seem unlike other exercises your children do at home or at school. So some children might seem reluctant to participate in imaginal journeys, or they may express difficulty imaging. In addition to respecting your child's hesitation to do such exercises, there are ways to stimulate the "imaginal muscle." To exercise the "imaginal muscle," I recommend the following books that have some very brief, introductory if you will, guided imaginal journeys that are great to start with: Richard de Mille's *Put Your Mother on the Ceiling*, Maureen Murdock's *Spinning Inward*, or Deborah Rozman's *Meditation for Children*. I will also offer some additional suggestions concerning this matter when the imaginal exercises themselves are presented.

WHAT ABOUT MUSIC?

There is a tribe in Africa whose members believe that music conjoins mysteriously with the mother, father, and the universe to conceive a child, to console him when hurt, to be her companion as she crosses the threshold of childhood into adolescence and budding adulthood, and to sustain him or her through all of life's crises and celebrations. Members of that tribe reckon a child's birthday from the first instant s/he appears as a sacred image in his mother's mind. As has been observed, the same day as the mother conceives of her child imaginally, she finds a quiet place beneath a shady tree where she waits until she can discern the song of her child. As if the universe had waited for this moment to bestow this gift, the mother apprehends the cosmic song of her child and returns to her village to share it with the man with whom she will conceive in flesh what already has been conceived in sound, tone, timbre, and rhythm. Together they sing that song as they make love, echoing the mystery of the universe and incarnating the music in the fetus that will grow in his mother's womb. The mother sings the song to her developing fetus and teaches it to the midwives who will help bring this life into the world. In fact, all of the villagers learn this song so they can help the child heal when he stumbles, or calm her when she cries. This song is also sung when the child goes through a rite of passage, when s/he marries, and finally, when s/he is about to die; so powerful is music that it cooperates with the forces of the cosmos to bring a child into this world and sustain him/her throughout life.[1]

Pythagoras believed that music helps to explain the secrets of healing human ailments and the secrets of the very structure of the universe. Indeed, there is great mystery, great potency, and great holiness in music. The Chasidic master Nachman of Bratslav taught that "through holy music you can come to the level of prophecy." The Rebbe taught that it is good to make a habit of inspiring oneself with a melody. "There are great concepts included in each holy melody," he claimed, "and they can arouse your heart and draw it toward God. Even if you cannot sing well, you can still inspire yourself with a melody sung to the best of your ability while alone at home. For the loftiness of melody is beyond all measure."

All spiritual traditions have a history of sacred music, from the Tibetan temple chants, to Chasidic *niggunim*, to the Gregorian chants. It was once absolutely natural to include music as an integral part of the spiritual life, yet there are those who believe we have lost that gift. A contemporary author and record producer, Joachim-Ernst Berendt, puts it this way: "The basic situation of modern man is being separated from nature, from the universe, from the other people. And there are just a few media to overcome this separation." He believes that meditation and love are two; the other is music, expressed especially through singing.[2]

To reclaim an ancient path to spirituality and evoke this feeling of unity in your children, I recommend that you consider music as a preparation for some of the spiritual exercises contained in this book. Children love to sing. When she thinks that I am not looking, my daughter often sings songs she has learned in school or songs she makes up as she goes along. Older children sing with the radio and with their favorite tapes or compact discs. With singing comes joy, self-expression, and often, a feeling of connection to others. Perhaps there is a song or melody that might serve as your call to the children to gather in your sacred space. It might be a song whose melody is repetitive and, thus, easily learned. As time goes on, the children might join with you in singing or humming this melody as they gather together for an exercise. Just think about it! What a wonderful way to join one heart to another and quiet the children's souls for a spiritual journey.

Rather than singing a song, you might wish to play instruments like a flute, a triangle, a drum, or any kind of instrument simple enough to include your children. Still another idea: play a record, cassette, or compact disc of evocative music. This might include Chasidic *niggunim*, Gregorian chants, Buddhist temple gongs, Indian ragas, or Tibetan temple music. Author David Carroll makes these recommendations: *Buddhist Drums, Bells and Gongs* (recording by Lyrichord); *Turkish Sufi Music* (Lyrichord); *Ancient Melodies* (Chinese sacred music, recording by Lyrichord); *Tibetan Temple Music* (Lyrichord).[3] Don Campbell, the founder and director of the Institute for Music, Health, and Education and one of the leading teachers of the healing potential of music (also known as sonic healing), has found that certain music helps concentration, relaxation, active imaging, or passive imaging. Based upon his research, Campbell makes these recommendations:[4]

1. To help concentration: Don Campbell's *Angels* (side 2), *Cosmic Classics, Crystal Meditations*; Eugene Friesen's *New Friends*; Mozart's *C Major Piano Concerto (Elvira Madigan)*; Ranier's *Songs of the Indian Flute*; Paul Winter's *Sunsinger*.

2. To help relaxation: Don Campbell's *Angels* (side 1), *Birthing, Crystal Rainbows, Runes*; Eno's *Music for Airports, The Pearl*; Kay Gardner's *The Rainbow Path*; Jonathan Goldman's *Dolphin Dreams*.

3. To help with active imagery: Beethoven's *Piano Concerto 5 in E Flat Major*; Brahms' *Violin Concerto in D Major*; Handel's *Royal Fireworks Suite*; Haydn's *Symphony 94 in G Major*; Mozart's *Symphony in C Major, Symphony in G Minor, Violin Concerto 5 in A Major*; Tchaikovsky's *Piano Concerto 1 in B Minor*.

4. To help with passive imagery: Don Campbell's *Dances for a Sleep-walker, Lightning on the Moon*; Corelli's *Concerto Grossi 4, 10, 11, 12*; Handel's *Water Music Suite*; David Hykes' *The Harmonic Choir*; Kitaro's *Silk Road*; Mascagni's *Intermezzo from Cavalleria Rusticana*; Satie's *Gymnopedies*; Vivaldi's *Flute Concertos*. (If you have trouble obtaining any of these recordings, Campbell offers his assistance. Write to him at the Institute for Music, Health, and Education, P.O. Box 1244, Boulder, CO 80306).

Experiment also with other classical compositions and various selections of ethnic music and folk songs that you find in your own search. Ask your children to indicate their choices. They will make it very clear which they like and which they don't.

WHY STORYTELLING IS IMPORTANT

Once upon a time there was a little boy and a mother who were driving in their car, when all of a sudden they crashed and had a terrible accident. Somehow the little boy was able to free himself from his seat and crawl out of the wrecked automobile. He did not know it, but the car was dangerously close to exploding—with his mother still inside! What he did understand, as young as he was, was that his mother was hurt and needed help. Heroically, he struggled to grab hold of his mother, and while chanting the mantra "I think I can, I think I can, I think I can," he dragged his mother out of the wreckage and up a small hill to safety.[5]

Once upon a time stories abounded. The greatest spiritual masters used them to conjure paradoxes to fool the logical minds of their disciples, to reframe the routine and educe new insights, to share the mysteries of the universe, and to convey the wisdom they had learned through the stories of their own masters. They knew that the most "entrancing words a language holds are 'Once upon a time . . . ,' that it is common to oppose truth but impossible to resist a story. Vyasa, the author of the sacred Hindu text the *Mahabharata*, says that if you listen carefully to a story you will never be the same again."[6] Actually, Nobel Prize-winning author Elie Wiesel has been known to claim that the appeal and power of tales is of such magnitude that God created humankind because He loves stories.

Historically, cultures around the world have turned to stories and their storytellers to teach a new generation about the values, the wisdom, the exemplars, and the visions of their people. These stories might be called myths, legends, parables, or fables. In Judaism the stories might be about the great early leaders Abraham or Moses, or about the pious rebbes like the Baal Shem Tov or Rebbe Nachman of Bratslav. Christians might tell about the life of Jesus and his disciples, or perhaps they might recount the just and loving deeds of St. Francis of Assisi or St. Thomas Aquinas. Buddhists might tell *jataka* tales about the earlier incarnations of the Buddha. Sufis might regale their children with wondrous stories about whirling dervishes or about the wisdom of the great Sufi master Bahaudin el-Shah.

Joseph Campbell once observed that "one of our problems today is that we are not well acquainted with the literature of the spirit."[7] While that may be a serious matter, it is not difficult to remedy. In addition to the great spiritual masters, the Irish had their *ollahms* and *shanachies,* the Jews had their *maggidim,* the Africans had their *griots,* the Norse had their *skalds,* the Anglo-Saxons had their *gleeman,* the French had their *troubadours,* as every people and every spiritual tradition had their own names for those who held the keys to the treasuries of spiritual tales. Yet one need not be among these masters to tell stories. In some magical, mysterious way, every parent has the capacity to be a storytelling master for his or her children.

What the world's great spiritual masters understood is what the little boy's act of courage exemplified: stories have great power. A story can reach deep into the heart and soul of a child, leaving behind a tender imprint that will last a lifetime. When I do storytelling workshops around the country, or even in Europe or Central America, inevitably the adults with whom I am sitting will recall a special story or two that they were told early in their lives. Sometimes these stories, first heard thirty or forty or fifty years ago or more, are recalled along with vivid recollections of who told them those stories, where they were sitting, what room they were in, and how they felt when they first heard those words: "Once upon a time." And the storytellers were almost always grandparents, parents, and older siblings.

Everyone can be a storyteller, and everyone can find a comfortable style for sharing stories. For some it is most natural to create their own stories; for others it might be most comfortable to recall incidents from their own lives or stories they heard in younger days. Some people like to read stories rather than tell them without a text in hand. Your own sense of what is right for you is the only guide you need. Even those who create their own tales or recall childhood incidents might want to read some of the wonderful stories I have assembled in the section at the back of the book entitled *Storytelling Resources*. These are all wonderful tales, some new and some very old, that help our children grow spiritually.

In addition to these recommended books, I would like to add some suggestions that I have found to be useful and successful when conducting storytelling workshops with parents, grandparents, teachers, and clergy:

1. The medieval Spanish Jewish sage, Moses ibn Ezra, taught that "words that come from the heart enter the heart." So delight in your stories and hold your children close or assemble them close to you. Read through the story before you tell it or read it so you can become familiar with it and, more importantly, so it can enter your heart.

2. Choose stories you like. It helps to transmit the spirituality, the wonder, the mystery, the insights, and the wisdom of your story if you are enchanted by it, too.

3. When it is possible, go to library storytelling sessions or to local/regional meetings of professional storytelling associations to watch others. Listen for the warmth and affection in the storyteller's tone and watch the open, embracing, welcoming body language as much as you pay attention to the actual words of the stories themselves.

4. Contact the National Association for the Preservation and Perpetuation of Storytelling (NAPPS, P.O. Box 309, Jonesborough, TN 37659. 615–753–2171) for general information, recommended book lists, and information about local/regional storytelling associations that may provide you with resources, mentors, and safe, secure places to do your own storytelling.

5. Form your own parents', grandparents', teachers', or clergy storytelling groups to enable you to swap information and tell stories.

6. Like the old bromide, "How do you get to Carnegie Hall?" to which the reply is "Practice, practice, practice," the best way to improve or feel comfortable as a person who tells stories to your children is to practice, practice, practice whenever you can.

7. If possible, find a fixed time and a special place for your storytelling and, thus, ritualize it daily.

8. As you become more comfortable with the exercises in this book, find your own ways to add stories to them. Trust your own sense of just the right story to prepare your children for a certain spiritual exercise or to extend the exercise and help process their experience.

9. The books I have recommended in the Storytelling Resource section may help give you ideas for follow-up activities to your storytelling. Let me add the personal caveat that sometimes the best ways to conclude a story include a good hug and kiss and some casual, spontaneous discussions from the heart about the tales.

Preparatory Exercises

PURIFICATION

An old saying has it that "cleanliness is next to godliness." Although some claim that this maxim has its origin in Jewish tradition, the connection between hygiene and spirituality has found its expression among religious traditions all around the world and throughout history. Customs based upon classical notions of purity and impurity are found among all known cultures and religions, whether modern or ancient, literate or preliterate, everywhere in the world.

Purification rituals are often preconditions for engaging in sacred rituals of many kinds. Sometimes they consist of only the simplest kind of hand or body washing, changing clothes, reciting a prayer or incantation, fumigating individuals with incense, or anointing them with some ritually pure substance. Some purification rituals go a bit further, however, and are known to involve purging, blood letting, and even beating.

Since the world in which we and our children live is filled with environmental, nutritional, emotional, and psychological pollutants, the need for purification is constant and complex. Later in this text I have some exercises that help us and our children detoxify our beings from some of the psychological and emotional pollutants that permeate our world. Specifically, the meditative exercises and Roberto Assagioli's "Technique of Evocative Words" found in Part Three help remove these kinds of toxins from our beings.

It is worthwhile, as well, to be careful about the foods our children eat. There are many professionals in our communities who can advise us about children's nutrition. There are also some books I would recommend and some newsletters to which you might subscribe. Here are some suggestions: *Natural Health, Natural Medicine* by Andrew Weil; *Target Recipes* by Covert Bailey and Lea Bishop; *The Macrobiotic Way* by Michio Kushi; *The Wellness Book* by Herbert Benson and Eileen Stuart; *Tufts University Diet & Nutrition Letter*; and the *University of California, Berkeley Wellness Letter.*

Of interest to us in this Part are the kinds of purification rituals that prepare our children's inner selves by cleansing their outer selves. Prior to enjoying some of the other spiritual exercises found in Parts Two and Three, I advise taking showers or baths. Consider bubble baths with aromatic oils. Children love bubble baths, and they often love to use loofah brushes to exfoliate their skin and invigorate the flow of blood and energy in their bodies. Let them play and, in their play, let them discover the feelings of renewal and rebirth that accompany cleansing.

In some cultures simply touching water is a purifying gesture, as we find in the *Vedas.* Merely gazing at water is considered to be purifying in Sri Lanka. Where water is unavailable in clean and ample supply clay, mud, wet herbs, or plants have been used. For some people, sweeping a house or some polluted area serves as a kind of purification ritual. There are those who use whisk brushes made of fibers from a symbolically pure source to cleanse their bodies. Others use steam baths or simply change into clean clothes, perhaps white clothes, to symbolize purity.

In Jewish tradition the early rabbis taught that carefulness leads to cleanliness that leads to purity that leads to humility that leads to saintliness. In a later age the noted Jewish author Michael Joseph Berdichevsky wrote that "washing your hands before a meal . . . is in itself a trivial act . . . but when you wash your hands by the command of God, . . . the souls of all the generations that lived and died to sanctify His name come into some kind of touch with you!"[8]

In his discussion of hygiene and its relationship to spirituality, author David Carroll reminds us that it is no coincidence that in Islam the devil is known as "the unclean one,"[9] and that Muslim and Hindu worshippers perform a ritual washing before praying. Of particular interest is Carroll's citation of a passage from a book called the *Sanatana Dharma* that was written to provide guidelines for raising Hindu children at the turn of this century. Among the contents of this text is a whole chapter on the concept of *shaucham* or bodily purity. There the author claims that neglect of one's bodily purity interferes with spiritual progress: "The purity of our higher energy body depends on the magnetic currents in it. It is quickly affected by the magnetic properties of surrounding objects, and we have therefore to be careful to be scrupulously clean."[10]

An act of ritual purification helps to prepare us and our children for spiritual exercises. Allow time for play, but also discuss what it feels like to be clean. Another thought: There are some spiritual teachers who recommend that prior to enjoying a purification ritual, a child might actually express his/her intention for doing that ritual. One might say, "I am washing my hands/taking this bath/brushing my body, etc., to cleanse myself outside and inside."

For those who have neither the time nor the inclination for full body cleansing, try these next two exercises with your children. It is my experience that if you do not anticipate resistance to these purification rituals, your children will participate naturally, following your example.

Exercise 1: Ritual Washing

PREPARATION

You will need a pitcher, a bowl, and a towel. Fill the pitcher with clean water. Bring these items to a quiet place or to the room you have established as your special spiritual place. You might wish to purchase a special pitcher, bowl, and towel to reserve for use only in this ritual. Shopping with your children in antique shops and in Asian or religious supply and gift stores might be a good way to find the items that "feel" like they belong in your personal purification ritual. Try some of the ethnic, religious, or relaxing music I have recommended or a cleansing incense like frankincense or myrrh to create an ambiance. Also, since purification is part of the world's religious traditions, you might want to investigate what prayer is said in your religious tradition prior to washing or ritual cleansing and read it before or after the exercise.

Take the pitcher in one hand and pour water over your other hand so that any spillage falls into the bowl. Then switch the pitcher to the other hand and repeat the procedure. When both hands have been washed take the towel and dry them off slowly and gently. Share the pitcher with any other participants. You may have to hold the pitcher and pour the water for small children who cannot hold it for themselves. Some children are more playful than others. Let them dangle their fingertips in the water bowl and enjoy the playfulness of the moment.

Once everyone has washed his/her hands you might wish to say a blessing, share a reading about purity and purification, or close your eyes and share a silent moment. I recommend that you try to maintain silence while each participant washes his/her hands, and observe the same procedure each time you perform this ritual.

Exercise 2: A Purification Visualization

PREPARATION

This exercise comes from the psychiatrist and renowned imaginal therapist Gerald Epstein and can be found in his popular book *Healing Visualizations*.[11] Unlike the previous exercise, this one requires no material preparation, and I would call it a somewhat advanced imaginal journey for most children. It may seem difficult for younger children, but then again it might not. Try it several times before you decide whether it is one you wish to incorporate into your children's spiritual practice. It employs many of the traditional tools and means of ritual purification that have been discussed. What follows is the script for the exercise. As is customary throughout the book, the script is here for you as a guide. I encourage you to become familiar with it so you can lead it in your own words. It may be too long for some young children or may employ words that are too difficult to understand. Feel free to make it your own and make adjustments to suit your children's needs.

INSTRUCTIONS

To begin, simply find your quiet place and sit comfortably. Close your eyes and breathe three times beginning with an exhalation. Make your exhalation the longer breath and your inhalation the shorter one. Then continue breathing normally.

Imagine you are leaving your home and going out into the street. (If you can imagine walking down a staircase, then do it.) Leave the street and see yourself descending into a valley, meadow, or garden, and go to the center of it. Find there a golden feather duster, whisk broom, or hand rake. With this tool, quickly clean yourself thoroughly from top to bottom, including your arms and legs. See how you look and feel, knowing that you have cleaned away all dead cells from the outside of your body and all gloom and confusion from the inside.

Put down the tool and hear the sound of a flowing stream or brook from your right. Go and kneel by its edge. Take the fresh, flowing, crystal clear, cool water in your cupped hands and splash it over your face, knowing that you are washing away all the impurities from the outside of your body. Then take the fresh, flowing, crystal clear, cool water in your cupped hands and drink it very slowly, knowing that you are washing away all the impurities from the inside of your body. Feel and sense yourself refreshed, tingling, energized, and more awake.

Get up from the stream and find a tree at the edge of the meadow. Sit under the tree that has branches hanging down with green leaves. With your back against the trunk, take in the pure oxygen coming from the leaves, together with the oxygen in the form of a golden blue light coming between the leaves from the sun and the sky. Breathe out carbon dioxide, the air inside your body, in the form of gray smoke which the leaves take up and convert into oxygen. This oxygen is given off by the leaves and comes from the trunk, entering your body through the pores in your skin. So, you are making a cycle of breathing with the tree and are breathing as one with the tree. Let your fingers and toes curl into the earth, like roots, and draw up energy. Stay there for a long moment, taking in what you need. Then get up from the tree and see how you look and feel.

Keep the image and feelings for yourself as you leave the garden and return to your street. Go back home the same way you went, and return to your chair. Then breathe out and open your eyes.

OTHER SUGGESTIONS

Experiment with other traditional means of ritual purification. Try baths and showers with special oils and cleansing incense or essential oils like frankincense, myrrh, cedarwood, and sandalwood. Try taking steam baths, using brushes made of special fibers, sweeping ritual spaces or cleaning sacred objects in those spaces, changing into special clothes, or using special cloths to wash hands and faces with Exercise 1. Most of all, accentuate the playfulness with children. When something they have done helps them to feel vital, renewed, fresh, open, receptive, and/or cleansed, you will know that this is the right kind of purification ritual for the time being.

BREATHING

Hopefully, by reading this book your children's spiritual awareness will be enhanced, and they will be led to a new and different way of seeing the world. Each act, each sight, each bit of perception of our world and our existence can offer them an experience of the transcendent—even the act of breathing. How many breaths have you taken while reading this book? Do you know that every breath bestows an opportunity to exercise spiritually? You do not need great amounts of money or elaborate equipment to do these exercises.

Jewish mystics have long connected the notion of breath (*neshimah*) to that of soul (*neshamah*). The great nineteenth-century Chasidic rebbe Nachman of Bratslav reinterpreted the Biblical verse, "The soul (*neshamah*) of man is a lamp of God" (Prov. 20:27), as meaning "the breathing (*neshimah*) of man is God's lamp." The medieval Jewish teacher Moses ben Maimon (Maimonides), a physician as well as a Torah scholar, believed that breathing influences our states of mind. More than seven centuries ago he speculated that changes in the quality of the air one breathes could lead to a change in the quality of one's mental activity, potentially manifesting itself symptomatically as mental confusion, poor comprehension, or diminished memory.

We certainly know from our own daily experience that our breathing and our states of mind are connected. For example, when we are upset or anxious we exhibit short and shallow breathing which results in a tightness across our upper chests. You can bet that the same is true for our children. On the contrary, watch a baby who is sound asleep, or pay attention to your own chest and abdomen when you are most relaxed. Ask your children to do the same. They will notice that their breath is long, fluid, effortless, and complete. Their chests and abdomens are expanded, and their bellies are nice and soft.

Thich Nhat Hanh, a very popular Vietnamese Buddhist teacher, speaks often about the fundamental connection between breathing and spirituality. "Our breath," he has said, "is the bridge from our body to our mind . . . [it] makes possible one-ness of body and mind."[12] Indeed, in Buddhist monasteries disciples learn to use their breath as a tool to stop mental dispersion and build up mindfulness.

Historically, the simplest and most basic kind of meditation concentrates on one's breath. The Sutra of Mindfulness (*Satipatthana Sutta*) teaches its disciples to be ever mindful of breathing in and breathing out: "Breathing in a long breath, you know, 'I am breathing in a long breath.' Breathing out a long breath, you know, 'I am breathing out a long breath.'"

Hindus traditionally have called the life energy *prana* and teach that it can be derived from the air we breathe. Baba Hari Dass believes that children, even as young as age three, can do simple yoga breathing exercises known as *pranayama*.[13] *Pranayama* is a terrific way to begin the day or a session of yoga exercises. Three of his *pranayama* exercises conclude this section on breathing.

Introducing our children to the mindfulness of breathing can help them in many different ways and in many different settings. When faced with upsetting or intimidating circumstances, breathing with mindfulness can dispel our children's fears and discomfort immediately. It engenders a calmness that brings confidence and security. And because each breath carries with it vital oxygen, deep and complete breathing can revitalize our children with dynamic energy whenever they need it.

Exercise 1: Mindfulness of Breathing

PREPARATION

The next exercises are designed to increase our children's mindfulness of their breathing and to begin to teach them how to connect their breathing with their inner states of being. Once they have practiced these exercises and are comfortable with them, encourage your children to use them as ways to quiet themselves before doing other kinds of spiritual exercises. At first, a minute or two may be the proper limit for their breathing session. Watch your children; they will let you know when enough is enough. Endeavor, however, to increase these breathing sessions to five minutes and eventually to fifteen or twenty minutes. You and your children will notice how these sessions bring rejuvenation and deep relaxation. Ask your children to dress comfortably in layers. As they become involved in these exercises, they might raise their body temperatures; they might be grateful at some point to have a shirt or sweatpants to remove. Also, have blankets, exercise mats, or round cushions available for your children to sit upon. It is possible for them to do these exercises either lying down or sitting up, with hands at their sides or upon their laps. Help your children experiment with body and hand positions to find what works best for them. Then read through the breathing exercises and revise the following scripts accordingly.

INSTRUCTIONS

Sitting (or lying comfortably), place your hands about three fingers below your navel. Rest your hands upon that section of your belly and abdomen. Breathe in slowly and as deeply as is comfortable and natural.

As you breathe in, feel your abdomen expand slowly as if a balloon were inflating inside your abdominal wall. Then gently and naturally allow yourself to exhale. Feel the abdomen (balloon) deflate. Breathe in again, slowly and as deeply as is comfortable. Feel your abdomen expand. Then exhale slowly and gently, and feel the abdomen deflate. Keep the breathing smooth, effortless, and flowing. (Repeat this simple activity for several minutes if you can. Keep restating the script. You might want to use an egg timer so you do not have to think of looking at a clock. Start with two or three minutes. That will seem long enough at the beginning. Eventually, if you wish, try to increase the time to ten, fifteen, or even twenty minutes. I guarantee your children will feel relaxed and invigorated.)

Exercise 2: Counting the Breath

PREPARATION

I based this exercise upon one I have heard Thich Nhat Hanh lead many times. It is a memorable experience to hear this gentle Zen master guide his audience in his soft, loving voice. For those who have not been blessed to be with him in person, Thich Nhat Hanh has included this and other Zen exercises in his book *The Miracle of Mindfulness.*

If your children have trouble counting, you may wish to choose another breathing exercise from this section. If, however, you select this for your children and they lose count at any time, simply tell them to return to 1 and start again. Help them not to judge themselves and not to compete with anyone, even themselves. Encourage them to enjoy the gift of life and the sensation of breathing.

INSTRUCTIONS

Breathe in and breathe out. Let your breath be light, even, and flowing like a thin stream of water running through the sand. Breathe in and breathe out. Feel the clean air enter your nose. How wonderful that feels! How clean! How pure! Breathe in and breathe out. Let your breath be quiet, so quiet that the person sitting next to you cannot hear it. Let your breath be long and easy. Feel your belly expand and get very soft. Breathe in and count 1 in your mind. Breathe out and count 1. Breathe in and count 2. Breathe out and count 2. Breathe in and count 3. Breathe out and count 3. Breathe in and count 4. Breathe out and count 4. Breathe in and count 5. Breathe out and count 5. Breathe in and count 6. Breathe out and count 6. Breathe in and count 7. Breathe out and count 7. Breathe in and count 8. Breathe out and count 8. Breathe in and count 9. Breathe out and count 9. Breathe in and count 10. Breathe out and count 10. Now breathe in and count 9. Breathe out and count 9. Breathe in and count 8. Breathe out and count 8. Breathe in and count 7. Breathe out and count 7. Breathe in and count 6. Breathe out and count 6. Breathe in and count 5. Breathe out and count 5. Breathe in and count 4. Breathe out and count 4. Breathe in and count 3. Breathe out and count 3. Breathe in and count 2. Breathe out and count 2. Breathe in and count 1. Breathe out and count 1. Then breathe out one last time. Feel how wonderful it is to breathe. Feel how alive, how energetic, and how pure you feel.

Exercise 3: Alternate Nostril Breathing

These three exercises are used by Baba Hari Dass. No special preparations are necessary.

1. Sit comfortably with legs crossed, spine erect, and hands lying limply upon the thighs or in a prayer pose. Inhale gently and deeply through both nostrils. Let the chest expand gently. Exhale just as gently. Feel the chest deflate. Repeat this several times.

2. Sitting comfortably, as before, close the right nostril with the thumb of your right hand and inhale gently and deeply through the left nostril. Then lift your thumb off the right nostril, close the left nostril with the fingers of your right hand, and exhale gently through the right nostril. Repeat this several times.

3. Close the left nostril with the thumb of your left hand and inhale gently and deeply through the right nostril. Then lift your thumb off the left nostril, close the right nostril with the fingers of your left hand, and exhale gently through the left nostril. Repeat this several times.

A Final Note

I would recommend that after the conclusion of any breathing exercises, you ask your children to remain seated for a moment or two, breathing normally. Ask them to notice how they feel. After centering this way, continue with your choice of spiritual exercises.

YOGA

Yoga is a Sanskrit word meaning "yoke." It is a method of training or discipline designed to lead to integration or union of one's Self with the Self of all Selves. Contrary to what many seem to believe, yoga is not a religion, and it does not demand subservience to a guru, a god, or a dogma.[14] Consequently, people of all religious backgrounds and philosophies can make use of yoga as a vehicle for spiritual development.

Classically, Hindus believe that there are four essential types of people, for whom there are four essential types of yoga, and any one of these can lead to the union of one's Self (*Atman*) with the Self of Selves (*Brahman*). The ancient texts speak of effecting this union through knowledge (*jnana yoga*), love (*bhakti yoga*), work/action (*karma yoga*), or psychological experiment (*raja yoga*).[15] However, all seekers are advised to cultivate specific habits to cleanse the mind and body as preliminary steps to any kind of yoga practice: noninjury, truthfulness, nonstealing, self-control, cleanliness, contentment, self-discipline, and a desire to reach the goal.

The kind of yoga exercises that follow are representative of *hatha yoga*. According to the scholar Huston Smith, *hatha yoga* originally served as preparation for the four classical types of yoga. He claims that, over the centuries, *hatha yoga* lost its connection to spirituality perhaps because it came to be considered a discipline in and of itself without any linkage to daily cleansing habits or devotion to one of the other forms of yoga.[16]

The word *hatha* is generally understood to mean "force" or "determined effort," so *hatha yoga* consists of sustained physical postures (*asanas*) meant to discipline the physical body, as well as breathing exercises (*pranayama*) that calm the nerves and increase the flow of life energy (*prana*). Baba Hari Dass explains that *hatha yoga* was developed and refined over centuries by those who sought to strengthen their bodies, maintain their flexibility, tone their internal organs and nervous systems, and relax their bodies and minds.[17] I have found yoga to be a wonderful way to prepare children's bodies and minds for all spiritual exercises.

GETTING READY

Breathing exercises (*pranayama*) are so much a part of yoga practice that you might want your children to begin and end their yoga sessions with some of the breathing exercises suggested earlier. In general, Baba Hari Dass suggests that postures be practiced before eating or at least three hours after a meal. However, a glass of water, juice, or milk is permissible before a session. Try to find a quiet, well-ventilated place free from wind , smoke, or dust. Indoors or outdoors, have some soft blankets or exercise mats available. If the space is chilly, ask your children to wear loose fitting, light clothing over tee shirts, shorts, or other exercise garb; if your children's body heat begins to rise, they can remove a layer of clothing for greater comfort.

Some of the postures (*asanas*) might be difficult for some children. Encourage them, but do not compel them to stretch or strain beyond their limitations. Remind them to breathe throughout, and never to hold the breath. Ask them to refrain from talking and to focus always on their breathing in and out. Grant your children permission to let you know when they are uncomfortable, and help create a secure and nonjudgmental environment in which all will want to try their best.

Here are four different sets of yoga postures (*asanas*) to try with your children or students. The first two are recommended by author and yoga instructor Barbara Milicevic.[18] The second two are recommended by yoga instructor Diane Avice du Buisson[19] using Baba Hari Dass's book. Any of these sets of exercises can be used before either indoor or outdoor spiritual practices. However, I recommend that you experiment with all of these postures to determine which best prepare you and your children for the various spiritual exercises found in this book.

Yoga Set 1

ARMS UP

After some breathing, sit cross-legged with hands either in prayer position or in the lap. Gently raise the arms to a sixty-degree angle. Keep the palms up as if trying to hold up the ceiling or sky. Hold this posture while breathing slowly and deeply. Begin with one-half to one minute. Then relax the arms gracefully, remain seated quietly, and continue to breathe slowly and deeply.

BOTTOMS UP

Lie on the back with knees propped up and apart. The arms are at the sides, touching or grabbing the ankles. Breathe slowly and deeply. Inhale, raising the buttocks up. Exhale, slowly coming down. Repeat, doing five to ten of these exercises. Relax quietly and continue to breathe slowly and deeply.

TRIANGLE POSE

Begin on all fours (hands and knees) and slowly raise the buttocks until you have formed a triangle shape. The legs and arms are straight. The bottom is up and the head hangs down. Try to keep the feet and hands flat on the floor, the weight equally distributed, and the kneecaps relaxed. Hold this posture for a count of 10 to 20, depending upon the age and condition of the student. Throughout the posture, breathe slowly and deeply. Come out of the posture gracefully, bending the knees, then sitting up on the heels. Relax quietly and continue to breathe slowly and deeply.

NECK ROLLS

Tuck the chin close to the chest, and then rotate it to the right. Make a slow, wide circle all the way around to the left shoulder and back to the center of the chest. Milicevic suggests telling your children to imagine that a pencil is pointing out of the top of their heads. Their aim is to

41

Arms Up

Triangle Pose

Bottoms Up

make as wide a circle as possible above them. Do this exercise several times, and then reverse the direction, rotating the head to the left several times. Relax quietly, and continue to breathe slowly and deeply.

Yoga Set 2

RAG DOLL BEND

Stand erect with arms stretched overhead to the ceiling or sky. Then slowly bend at the waist, letting the upper torso drop; shoulders, arms, everything should be limp. Do not force anything. Do not strain. However, do not let the knees bend too much. Then, slowly stand up using the strength in the legs. Relax quietly while standing comfortably and breathing slowly and deeply.

SIDE BENDS

Stand comfortably and quietly. Spread the feet about one foot to one and one-half feet apart and bend sideways from the waist, sliding the left arm down the side and extending the right arm straight up. Hold the pose for a count of 5 and slowly change sides. Relax quietly while standing comfortably and breathing slowly and deeply.

COW-CAT POSE

Stand comfortably and quietly. Come down on all fours (hands and knees) and lift the head up as if gazing at the ceiling or sky. This is the cow pose. Inhale as the head is lifted. Then exhale and bring the chin down on the chest and arch the back up like a cat. Do this several times, alternating cow and cat, inhaling and exhaling. Then come down and relax quietly on the stomach. Continue to breathe slowly and deeply.

COBRA POSE

While relaxing on the stomach, breathe slowly and deeply. Put the legs together and the hands flat down at either side of the shoulders on the

Rag Doll
Bend

Side Bends

Cow Cat

Cobra

floor or ground. Slowly raise the head up to look at the ceiling or sky, bringing the shoulders and chest up. Straighten the arms and hold for five to ten seconds. Slowly return to the floor or ground, keeping the head up until the very last. Then relax on the stomach quietly while breathing deeply and slowly.

Yoga Set 3

PALM TREE

Stand comfortably and quietly, breathing slowly and deeply. Put your feet together, and let your arms hang easily at your sides. Lift the right arm high above the head. Rise up on the toes, and at the same time stretch the left arm down. Hold this pose for three to five seconds. Imagine you are a giant palm tree. Breathe slowly and deeply at all times. Now raise your left arm and repeat this *asana*. Then try with both arms above your head. Reach high. Then return to standing position, and rest comfortably. Breathe slowly and deeply.

FLAT ON THE FLOOR

Stand comfortably and quietly, breathing slowly and deeply throughout the exercise. Place your feet about a hip's width apart. Bend down slowly and gently. Touch the floor with your palms if you can; otherwise, bend forward as much as is comfortable. Do not force or strain. Then stand up slowly, letting the strength of your legs help you. Return to standing position. Rest comfortably, and breathe slowly and deeply.

BOW

Stand comfortably and quietly, breathing slowly and deeply. Lie down on your stomach upon the floor or ground. Move slowly, and continue to focus on your breathing. Bend your legs and lift your feet off the floor. Reach back and grab your feet or ankles with your hands and hold your legs close to you. Look up at the ceiling or sky. Now pull on your

Thunderbolt

Palm Tree

Tree

Bow

Rest Pose

feet, lifting your knees off the floor, and stretch like a bow. Come down slowly, letting your legs back down. Rest comfortably on the floor with your head rolled to one side and your arms lying at your sides. Breathe deeply and slowly.

CAT

This *asana* is called the "cow-cat" in Set 2 of the yoga postures. Instead of coming down on all fours, come up upon all fours from lying on the stomach and proceed as instructed above.

COBRA

Rest comfortably upon the floor or ground. This posture is included in Set 2, as well. Proceed as instructed above.

THUNDERBOLT

Rest comfortably upon the floor or ground. Breathe slowly and deeply. Come to a kneeling position and sit back upon your heels. Put your hands, palms down, upon your knees and take a few slow and deep breaths.

REST POSE

Now lie down on your back. Keep your arms at your sides and your feet slightly apart. Roll your head to one side. Close your eyes and relax in this rest pose. Breathe deeply and slowly. Rest comfortably and quietly. When you are ready to release this pose, open your eyes and roll gently onto one side. Stay there for just a moment. Then raise your body into a sitting pose that is comfortable. Sit with your eyes open and your body relaxed for just a moment. Continue to breathe deeply and slowly. Notice how your body feels. When you are ready, stand up and end this set of postures.

Yoga Set 4

SALUTE TO THE SUN

This is actually a collection of twelve separate poses choreographed as one and labeled with letters so as not to be confused with the sets themselves. Do the poses consecutively, but please remember to breathe deeply and slowly at all times. Do not strain or force. This is a wonderful exercise to do anytime, anywhere, but I believe it is especially powerful to do outdoors early in the morning as the sun is rising or later in the day as it is setting.

SALUTATION POSE

Stand comfortably and quietly. Breathe slowly and deeply. Observe the world around you. Look at the magnificence of the sunlight. Place your palms together in front of your heart, fingers pointing upward in prayer or salutation pose.

UPWARD SALUTATION POSE

Stretch your arms up over your head, keeping your hands together, and bend back as far as you can.

HANDS TO FEET POSE

Bend forward and place hands on the floor beside your feet (or as far as you can reach). Keep your legs straight and try to touch your forehead to your knees.

ONE FOOT EXTENDED POSE

Keeping palms flat on the floor or ground, stretch your left leg straight back and bend your right knee in front of your chest. Rest your left knee on the floor or ground, and look up.

BOTH FEET EXTENDED POSE

Bring the right leg back to meet the left (resembling push-up position). Try to keep only the hands and feet in touch with the floor or ground, and your head, back, and legs in a straight line.

EIGHT LIMBS BOWING POSE

Lower the body to the floor or ground gently. Rest there with the buttocks slightly lifted as if bowing prone in salutation.

SNAKE POSE

Raise the head and shoulders off the floor or ground by straightening your arms in front of you. Bend your head back, keeping the shoulders raised. Look up at the ceiling or sky.

MOUNTAIN POSE

Raise your buttocks, keeping your arms and legs as straight as possible. Keep your head down; try to touch your heels to the floor. Your body looks like an upside-down "V," a mountain. Imagine you have become a mountain. Feel your quiet strength and majesty.

ONE FOOT EXTENDED POSE

Bring your left foot forward between your hands, keeping your right leg stretched back. Look up at the ceiling or sky.

HANDS TO FEET POSE

Bring your right foot up to meet the left. Make your legs straight and try to touch your forehead to your knees.

UPWARD SALUTATION POSE

Raise your arms up over your head, hands together as you did at the beginning of these exercises, and bend back as far as you can.

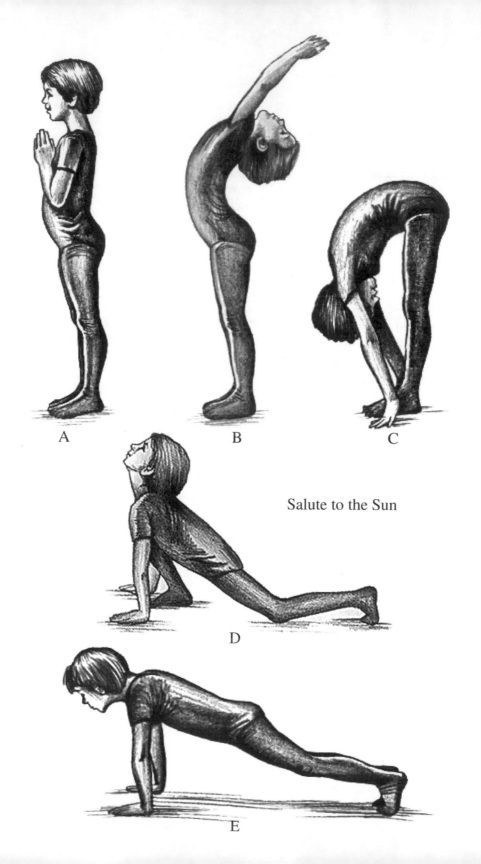

A   B   C

Salute to the Sun

D

E

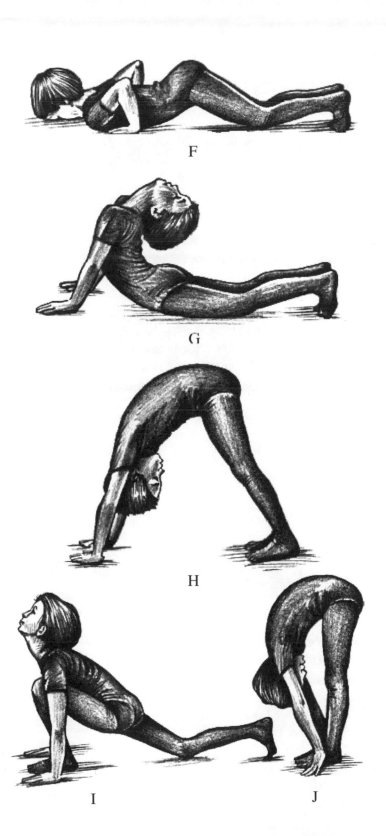

F

G

H

I   J

SALUTATION POSE

Lower your arms and straighten your back. As you did at the beginning, place your palms together in front of your heart. Stand comfortably and quietly. Breathe deeply and slowly. Notice how the different parts of your body feel.

If you are up to it, finish Set 4 with the next three *asanas*. If not, go right to the rest pose at the end of this set.

TREE POSE

Stand comfortably with your feet together and your arms at your sides. Breathe deeply and slowly. Put the sole of your left foot on the inside of your right leg, as high up on your thigh as possible. Rotate your knee out to the side. Arms go above your head with palms together, fingers pointing upward. Try to balance for three to five seconds. Then reverse legs and repeat. Finally, lower your arms and leg. Stand comfortably and quietly. Breathe deeply and slowly.

CAT POSE

As in Set 3 of the *asanas*.

THUNDERBOLT POSE

As in Set 3 of the *asanas*.

REST POSE

As in Set 3 of the *asanas*.

NOTES

1. Jack Kornfield, "A Parent's Guide to Conscious Childraising: Conscious Parenting," *Common Boundary* 2 (January/February 1993): 23.

2. Joachim-Ernst Berendt, "Where Has All the Singing Gone," *Utne Reader* (September/October 1991): 47.

3. David L. Carroll, *Spiritual Parenting* (New York: Paragon House, 1990), p. 238.

4. Don G. Campbell, *Music: Physician for Times to Come* (Wheaton, IL: Quest Books, 1991), pp. 252–53.

5. Steven M. Rosman, "The Power of Story," *Hadassah Magazine* (January 1992): 32.

6. Anthony de Mello, *The Heart of the Enlightened: A Book of Story Meditations* (New York: Doubleday Books, 1989), p. 7.

7. Ernest Kurtz and Katherine Ketcham, *The Spirituality of Imperfection: Modern Wisdom from Classic Sources* (New York: Bantam Books, 1992), p. 8.

8. Michael Joseph Berdichevsky, "Din uDebarim," in *Hebrew Reborn*, ed. S. Spiegel (New York: Macmillan Co., 1930), p. 372.

9. Carroll, p. 198.

10. Carroll, p. 199.

11. Gerald Epstein, "The Garden of Eden," in *Healing Visualizations* (New York: Bantam Books, 1989), pp. 198–99.

12. Thich Nhat Hanh, *The Miracle of Mindfulness: A Manual on Meditation* (Boston: Beacon Press, 1987), p. 23.

13. Baba Hari Dass, *A Child's Garden of Yoga* (Santa Cruz, CA: A Sri Rama Publishing/Hanuman Fellowship Book, 1980), p. 6.

14. Dass, p. 11.

15. Huston Smith, *The Religions of Man* (New York: HarperPerennial, 1986), p. 46.

16. Smith, p. 47.

17. Dass, p. 14.

18. Barbara Milicevic, the author of *Your Spiritual Child*, has been a yoga instructor for many years. She has also taught reading and writing on the college level, integrating principles of self-empowerment in all her lessons. When working with children, she often uses meditation and yoga to help guide them to self-mastery and self-expression, and she has been known to proclaim with pride that her own children have been her best teachers.

19. Diane Avice du Buisson has been a student of *hatha* and *ashtanga yoga* for fourteen years. She has studied with masters all over the contiguous United States, Hawaii, and in South Africa. She has taught yoga to delighted pupils here and abroad.

Part Two

Going Outside

Conducting Spiritual Exercises Outdoors

"What is life? It is the flash of a firefly in the night. It is the breath of a buffalo in the winter time. It is the little shadow which runs across the grass and loses itself in the Sunset."

Crowfoot

"Let a man once begin to think about the mystery of his life and the links which connect him with the life that fills the world, and he cannot but bring to bear upon his own life and all other life that comes within his reach the principle of reverence for life..."

Albert Schweitzer

There may be no better expert in the field of nature education than Joseph Cornell. His books *Sharing Nature with Children* and *Sharing the Joy of Nature* are classics and fundamental reading for anyone interested in helping children grow spiritually through encounters with the natural world.

Cornell's basic tenets of nature education include: share your inner feelings about what you may see, hear, feel, taste, or touch with your children; share your feelings of awe and respect with them, as well; be in the moment with your children by really listening to them and being aware; focus the child's attention, and set the tone for the experience right away; don't subject your children to explanations before they see and experience the natural world directly; talk about what was seen after it has been experienced; don't worry about knowing the precise names of every plant, tree, animal, or insect; allow a sense of joy and delight to permeate the experience.[1]

The following two exercises come from Cornell's book *Sharing the Joy of Nature.* They encourage an appreciation of the natural world and help children bring their attention to the wonders of a world that is suffused with magic in the midst of the mundane.

Outside Exercises

Tree Imagery

"Now I see the secret of making the best persons. It is to grow in the open air and sleep with the earth." So said Walt Whitman a century ago. It seems to me that the passing of years has not rendered this wisdom outdated. However, many children do not spend much time outdoors anymore. Computer games, videos, and MTV capture them and their time. Few of them feel the rhythm of nature or feel organically connected to the flora and fauna that surround our cities, our homes, and our office buildings.

PREPARATION

The first exercise in this section grants our children a chance to sense the rhythm of the natural world as it reverberates in their souls. It can be practiced indoors or outdoors. To begin, gather the participants together and explain to them that they are about to experience the life of a tree for a whole year: summer, fall, winter, and spring. In a manner of speaking, they are actually going to become trees in their imaginal realms. Children who wish can hold their arms up like branches, or they can simply stand still. Allow the children to sway or move as the narrative suggests.

As I recommend before leading any exercise in this book, read through the narrative and make any changes necessary to best meet the needs and abilities of the children participating. You may find this narrative a bit long, so abbreviate it as you see fit. Yet I have done this exercise with very young primary age children who participated in the entire exercise nicely. Since all children are unique, maybe your children will do best if you choose, for example, to end the imaginal journey after summer or after autumn. Maybe you will choose to end the exercise before the reading of the subsequent poem. I advise that if you abbreviate this exercise to best meet the needs of your children, invite them to remain standing still with their eyes closed. Encourage them to breathe deeply and comfortably. Try to extend the life of the images in their minds by requesting that they be very still and think about everything they have imagined and all of the experiences they sensed during whatever part of the exercise they did. For those who are abbreviating this exercise, some quiet moments using some of my recommendations will provide a nice gentle conclusion to the exercise. It is always possible to add additional parts slowly until your children are comfortable with the entire imaginal exercise.

Also, this exercise may include words that are unfamiliar to your children. These can be explained beforehand, or other words can be substituted for them. Because the exercise offers a detailed description of the anatomy of a tree, you might also want to get a good picture or drawing to show your children to familiarize them with specific details before you begin.

As much as possible, make the words of the narrative yours and speak them naturally. Join the children and become a tree yourself. In addition to demonstrating your respect and appreciation for the exercise by participating, you might grow closer to that glorious realm of leaves and lazy breezes without even going on vacation.

INSTRUCTIONS

(With the children standing under a tree either holding their arms up like branches or simply standing still with their hands at their sides, begin the guided imagery.) Here is the narrative:

Close your eyes....

Trees are very important to life on Earth. They create half the world's oxygen. They hold the soil and prevent erosion. They provide food and shelter for untold billions of animals. They warm their immediate environment in winter and cool it in the summer with their shade. Trees inspire us with thoughts of beauty, nobility, strength, and serenity.

With your eyes closed, in your mind see yourself walking through a forest of large deciduous trees. (Pause.) Now you are entering a clearing in the middle of the forest. Stop, turn toward the sun, and feel yourself becoming a large tree in this forest.

Stand with your feet a shoulder's distance apart and feel your huge taproot growing down from your hips. Feel it go down through your thighs . . . your knees . . . and down through your ankles . . . down through the soles of your feet and into the earth. Your taproot is working itself through the soft topsoil and working farther down, down, deep into the clay soil. Keep sinking your taproot farther and farther down into the earth until it's over thirty feet deep. (Pause.)

Now begin sending lateral roots out in all directions, just beneath the surface of the ground. Send them out to the left . . . to the right . . . in front . . . and behind. Spread them out farther and farther—ten feet, twenty feet, past thirty feet from the trunk. (Pause.)

Gently sway back and forth. Feel how firmly you're rooted in the earth. (Pause.) Mentally look at your large trunk and see how big and round you are. (Pause.) Is your bark smooth or rough? Is it dark or light colored? (Pause.)

Now follow your trunk up higher and higher until you come to your biggest branches. Follow them as they divide into smaller and smaller branches and spread out into the sky.

It's summertime, and life is easy. The days are long. The sun is warm. A light breeze blows your branches gently back and forth. Feel how your roots hold you firmly anchored to the earth.

What kind of leaves do you have? Are they large and pointed? Or are they small and round?

Absorb energy from the sun's warm rays. Bring it into your leaves and make food, using sunlight, air, and the water that you've brought up from the ground. Now send the food you've made in your leaves down through your branches to your trunk. Feel it going down, down, all the way to your roots. Store it there. Summer is the time when you store food. (You stopped growing many months ago, before the end of spring.)

Deep in the earth, gather water from the soil using your tiny root hairs. Your root hairs spread out and touch nearly every particle of soil around you. Bring this moisture up. Feel it rise first in tiny streams, then as vast rivers of moisture. Now it's surging up the trunk, racing higher and higher up the trunk at speeds up to a hundred miles per hour, and then out through the branches and into the leaves. Now it evaporates from your leaves, permeating the atmosphere all around you with moisture. As autumn approaches, the days grow short and the sunlight is less intense. Food production finally comes to a complete halt. It's getting cooler, and the sap in your leaves is starting to descend, down, out of your branches and into your trunk, and down to your roots below. There, deep in your roots, the sap is stored for next spring.

Watch as your abandoned leaves turn gold, yellow, or red. What is happening is not new—you've dropped your leaves in autumn many times through the years. Cast off your leaves and become dormant now. You are preparing yourself, protecting yourself from the approaching cold of winter. (Pause.)

Storm clouds come rolling over the horizon, darkening the sky. The wind begins to push at your upper branches. The rain patters in big drops and then pounds at your naked branches with their few remaining leaves. A fierce wind rips through the forest and tears off many leaves, driving them to the ground. Look down at the forest floor. It's covered with your brightly colored leaves and leaves from the trees around you. (Pause.) The storm breaks, and your branches are completely soaked. Hear the water drip from limb to limb on its way to the ground. (Pause.)

Winter isn't over yet. An even bigger storm blows in from the sea. Listen to the roar of its approach. Powerful gusts rattle your branches and toss them about. Like a ship on an angry sea, you rock back and forth, back and forth, back and forth. Only your big taproot and large lateral roots keep you from crashing to the ground.

The storm is beginning to blow itself out. The wind is slackening. Once more, the forest is quiet. Your branches are almost bare now, and the ground is painted gold, yellow, and red. Your stark silhouette stands out against the somber gray winter sky. One by one, your last leaves fall off and gently roll and tumble to the earth. The temperature drops, and snow begins to fall. Feel the snow as it piles up on your branches.

All animal life has left the forest. Many of the insects have died. Most of the birds have flown south. The mammals are either hibernating or have gone down to the warmer valleys. You, too, have died to only one percent of your living tissue—to a thin thread of life just inside your bark. (Pause.)

But already stored in your tiny buds are next year's leaves and flowers. See them on the tips of your branches, protected from the cold and wet of winter by a waxy sheath. These buds are your new life for the coming year. Crouch down. Kneel down and become a tiny leaf bud. You're like a baby in its mother's womb, waiting for your time, waiting for spring. (Pause.)

The days are becoming longer and warmer. When the temperature and sunlight are just right, the sap deep in the tree's roots awakens and surges up through the trunk, racing higher and higher, emerging into the branches and entering the buds. (Pause.) Unfold now as a tiny, tender, bright green, spring leaflet. Open up completely to the spring sun and receive its warming, energy-giving rays. Feel the sun's energy and nourishment, and grow green, grow large.

Send food energy down to the rest of the tree. Now, feel all the leaves in one branch and give the vitality you feel from the sun to the tree.

Become the whole tree again. Feel your roots as they reach deeper into the earth. (Pause.) Feel the tips of your branches growing. You are growing from both ends—and a little around the middle! Spring is the time of renewal. Now ninety-nine percent of your body has come back to life, adding tremendous vitality to you and to the forest.

With your renewal, animals and plants return to the forest. Birds land in your branches. Reach out with one of your branches and let a robin land on you. Deer are feeding around your trunk. Wildflowers are pushing up and out from the earth beneath you. All animal life depends upon you for food, shelter,—and, yes, even a sense of well-being. Spread your branches out to all living things in the forest, in a spirit of protection and love. Feel that you share one life together, in beauty and harmony. (Pause.)

Please lie down on your back. I'm going to read a poem about a tree. Feel that you're becoming part of the tree that each line describes. After the first stanza, you can open your eyes and look at the base of a large tree. (Pause and make it clear that you are about to begin the poem.)

Roots going down,
reaching
through damp earth deep.
Down, down,
holding me here.

Open your eyes
and look at the trunk
of a large tree . . .

My great round trunk,
massive and slender,
solid yet yielding,
carrier of life.

My long limbs
stretching out for space,
tips tickled by the wind,
touched by the sun.

They invite all life
to shelter among them,
beneath them, inside me,
beneath me.

Life runs through me.
I invite all life to me.

Roots anchored deep,
limbs lofty high,
I abide in both worlds
of earth and sky.

I have found that this is a good time to allow your children just to
be as they are. Permit them to get up when they wish, but also invite
them to stay lying down looking at the trees and the sky to their hearts'
content.

Camera

Rachel Carson once said, "If a child is to keep alive his inborn sense of wonder without any such gift of the fairies, he needs the companionship of at least one adult who can share it, rediscovering with him the joy, excitement and mystery of the world we live in." This exercise, which Joseph Cornell calls "Camera," grants children the sacred opportunity to discover the joy and mystery of our world with your companionship.

PREPARATION

There is no script for this exercise. Bring along some large index cards (five-by-eight) and some crayons or magic markers so the person-camera can draw one or two of the pictures s/he recalls best from the day's photo session.

INSTRUCTIONS

Here is the way you play the game: One person will play the role of the photographer, and one will be the camera. The photographer guides the camera on an expedition through natural terrain near or far. The camera keeps his/her eyes closed as the photographer searches for a special picture of any natural phenomenon. The photographer is free to aim the camera using any angle that might best capture the essence of the subject under scrutiny.

Once the photographer finds something s/he wants to photograph, s/he aims the camera and taps the shoulder of his/her companion-camera to open the lens and "take" the picture. Allow the camera about five seconds or so to take in whatever his/her eyes first see. Then tap the shoulder of the camera a second time to close the lens until the photographer finds another picture to take.

After the photographer has taken several pictures, it is time to "develop" the film. Use the large index cards and the crayons or magic markers you have brought along so the camera can draw one or two of the pictures s/he recalls best from the day's photo session. Then switch roles so the photographer now becomes the camera.

Try unusual camera angles. Photograph looking straight up at a tree or around a corner. Capture dew drops on leaves, insects amidst their daily routines, sunsets and sunrises, deer in the woods, and even wind blowing through trees.

Cornell advises that parents, teachers, or other adult guides may want to spend some time showing the children how to guide their "blind" cameras (siblings, friends, or classmates) sensitively and protectively. It is my experience that gently steering their shoulders works best. Also, Cornell explains that this exercise works especially well when it is done in silence.

Growing Seed Meditation

The great naturalist John Muir once said, "Every natural object is a conductor of divinity." In this exercise, children have a chance to behold the divine miracle of growth as it occurs in the life of a sprouting bean or seed. Children are more acutely aware of growth than we are sometimes. They know when they have grown too big for this dress, those pants, or those shoes. They know when Tommy is bigger or Jimmy is smaller. They also have pets in their homes or classrooms, and they know when Spot is getting bigger.

Whereas things, animals, and our children themselves might be growing, there is not as specific an organic connection to growth as there can be with nature. It is one thing that Spot grows, but your child did not give birth to Spot. Helping to give birth to the sprouts that emerge from beans can lead to a sensation of nurture that simply does not come with Spot's growth. Also, we and our children tend to notice incidentally that someone or something has grown. We do not spend time daily observing the miracle of growth, of life sprouting before our eyes—life we helped to germinate.

It is a wonder to watch growth slowly. It is a blessing to feel an organic connection to a living thing that the touch of your hands helped the universe create. People may mock those whose lives are said to move so slowly or who seem so inactive that they are thrilled "watching grass grow." Yet that grass grows at all, that flowers bud, that shoots sprout, and that trees blossom are miracles available to our children everyday. The miracle of the universe is contained in every seed; in this case, it is contained in every bean.

PREPARATION

Below I have included two different ways to observe the wonder of germination that I learned from my mother-in-law, Norma Ziegel, a fabulous early childhood educator. Look them over and choose one you like. Perhaps you will like them both; then use them both. The only thing that could be more divine than observing one example of the miracle of growth would be to observe two examples. These projects are the foci of the following spiritual exercise and not the exercise itself.

INSTRUCTIONS

1. Place a wet paper towel into a plastic bag. Put a lima bean into the middle of the wet towel. Close the bag and put it in a dark place until the bean begins to split open. This may take three days or more. Once the bean has begun to open up, take it out of its dark resting place and hang it in its plastic bag on the inside of a window. Make sure to keep the paper towel moist, but not too wet, as the sprouts grow.

—OR—

2. Take a plastic bag and punch holes in its bottom with a pin. Place about fifteen to twenty sprouting seeds (e.g., mung beans or alfalfa sprouts) in the bag. Close the bag and put it in a tray of warm water overnight. The next morning drain the bag, rinse the seeds, and put the bag in a warm spot in your home. Repeat this for two more days. After rinsing the seeds on the fourth morning, place the bag in a sunny location so the sprouts will turn green.

Once sprouts have begun to emerge from either the lima bean or the seeds, you are ready to use your germinating bean or seeds as the focus of a meditation. Hang the plastic bag from a window pane so your children might observe the seeds or bean and still see some of the outside world peripherally.

To enrich your exercise environment, you might want to burn some incense or diffuse some oil in the room about one-half hour ahead of time. Myrrh, sandalwood, or frankincense are among the scents that help cleanse a site and facilitate openness to an exercise. Also, I like to play music softly as an undertone to this exercise. Carroll and Campbell have some recommendations that we reviewed in Part One. You may have a choice of your own. Hopefully, this will not be the last time you do this exercise, so you can experiment without the pressure of having to choose the "perfect" music or incense. You may also choose to use neither music nor incense for this exercise; these are merely my suggestions.

Many children may not be able to visualize the seed or the sprouts in their imaginations. That's okay. As I have observed, our visualization or imaginal "muscles" do not get much exercise in our society. It takes a while to get them strong enough to be able to create and hold an image. Rather than have any child feel s/he has failed, ask him/her to close his/her eyes and feel the seed and its sprouts in the plastic bag. Feel the contours. Feel the texture. Do so nice and slowly so each little nook and bump is noticed. You might also ask your children to draw what they see. Observe the growth of your seed at least once a week. From time to time, ask your children to attempt to see the seed and its sprouts in their imaginations. But do not let them get discouraged. They can always feel the seed with their eyes closed and/or draw the seed and its sprouts, noting changes in growth from week to week.

INSTRUCTIONS

This is a scripted meditative exercise. As with any of the other scripted exercises, read it through carefully and make any adaptations necessary for your children.

Look at the seeds (or bean). Find the one that you like most. Trace its contours with your eyes. Trace its sprouts. Just let your eyes act like a pencil or a crayon. Outline this seed and its sprouts with your eyes. Move slowly, without rushing. You have all the time you need. Notice the shape of the seed. Is it round? Are some parts sharp? Notice its color. Is it dark or light? What color does it seem to resemble most? Notice its surface. Is it smooth or bumpy? Notice its sprouts. Do they emerge from the top or the bottom of the seed? How many sprouts can you count? What do they look like?

Now close your eyes if that is okay for you. Do you see any part of the seed or its sprouts? Open your eyes, and look at the seed and its sprouts again. Look closely, so when you close your eyes, you will be able to draw parts of the seed and its sprouts in your imagination. Now, close your eyes. Try your best to draw the seed and its sprouts in your imagination. Remember its colors. Remember its shape. Remember its size. Remember where the sprouts grow out of the seed. Remember anything you can. Whatever you remember is all you need.

Try to do this exercise at least once a week until the seed has sprouted sufficiently to plant it in some soil. Ask the children to note whatever changes in growth they perceive. Eventually, invite them to help you plant the seed in a pot. It is valuable for them to maintain their connection with a seed they have raised from birth through its various stages of life.

The Name Game

Thich Nhat Hanh has talked many times about the importance of calling things by their names. I have heard him recall mealtimes when he has picked up a piece of tofu and called it "tofu," to put himself more in touch with the food he was going to eat. Part of the practice of mindfulness is to make things more real by calling them by their names.

This lesson reminds me of the Biblical narratives of the Garden of Eden. After Adam was created, God granted him permission to name the other creatures that coexisted with him in the Garden. In their inimitable midrashic[2] style, the early rabbis imagined that God not only gave Adam the privilege of naming the birds, the insects, the fish, and the beasts of the field, but also gave him the opportunity to name himself and, believe it or not, to call God by a name.

What a powerful spiritual message! From the very first moments of our birth in the universe, our children have been given a fundamental key to the spiritual life; that is, they can become mindful of every aspect of the cosmos by calling everything and everyone they encounter by name. Thus, when they pick up a flower and say, "rose," they no longer hold merely a botanical entity. It is a rose they hold, and they can begin to know it, to appreciate it, and to value it by stepping beyond the barrier of anonymity. They might deepen their encounter by getting in touch with the details of that specific rose: "It is not just any rose. This rose I hold in my hands has pink petals. It is soft and has its own fragrance. This pink rose seems young and ready to blossom (or it seems old and withered). It is one of many roses that share the same vine (or it sits by itself, alone and independent)."

The next exercise is called "The Name Game" because it asks your children to spend time getting to know some of the animate and inanimate creations that share the journey around the sun with them on this spaceship we call Planet Earth.

PREPARATION

To begin, choose a preparatory exercise from the previous section. Then go outside to the grounds around your home or school or to a park in your neighborhood. Assign each child a couple of square yards of ground. Give each child a few pieces of paper and a box of crayons/markers/colored pencils. I have found it helpful to have a book or two for identifying common plants, stones, and insects. I think that you develop a different relationship with someone or something when you are on a first name basis.

While bookstores and libraries abound with resources that are good and easily found, here are some books to try: *A Child's Book of Insects* by Kathleen N. Daly (New York: Doubleday & Company, 1977); *Insects All Around Us* by Richard Armour (New York: McGraw-Hill Book Company, 1981); *Insect* by Laurence Mound (New York: Alfred A. Knopf, 1990); *Wildflowers and The Stories Behind Their Names* by Phyllis S. Busch (New York: Charles Scribner & Sons, 1977); *Look at a Flower* by Anne Ophelia T. Dowden (New York: Thomas Y. Crowell Company, 1963); *The Visual Dictionary of Plants* (New York: Darling Kindersley, Inc., 1992); *Secrets in Stone* by Gerald Ames (New York: Four Winds Press, 1970).

INSTRUCTIONS

Tell all of the participants that they will have fifteen minutes (for younger children) to one-half hour (for older children) to draw everything they see in their areas. That means everything: dirt, rocks, pebbles, grass, weeds, flowers, plants, insects, sticks, leaves, birds, sand, gravel, etc. Make sure that everything drawn is labeled with its proper name. Children who cannot write will need help labeling what they have drawn. Flowers ought not be labeled merely as flowers if you or the child knows their proper names. Insects, leaves, birds, plants, and even rocks ought to be labeled specifically also, if the names are known. Ask the children to touch and smell any of the objects they feel comfortable touching and smelling.

When the time has elapsed, gather the children together. Ask the children to tell you about what they discovered in their areas. Ask them about the textures and the fragrances of their objects. What colors were the objects or things? Invite them to show you and talk about what they have drawn.

You might want to conclude this exercise by reading one of the following stories or any story you know that expresses a wonder of nature. I suggest: *When Light Turns into Night* by Crescent Dragonwagon (New York: Harper & Row, 1975), ages four to seven; *Mr. Tamarin's Trees* by Kathryn Ernst (New York: Crown Publishers, Inc., 1976), ages five to eight; *Something for the Medicine Man* by Flora Mae Hood (Chicago: Melmont Publishers, Inc., 1962), ages seven to ten; *In Search of a Sandhill Crane* by Keith Robertson (New York: The Viking Press, Inc., 1973), ages eleven and up; *Grandmother Lucy in Her Garden* by Joyce Wood (New York: Collins-World, 1975), ages four to eight. Also, Joseph Cornell recommends *The Man Who Planted Hope and Grew Happiness* by Jean Giono (Brooksville, Maine: Friends of Nature, 1967).

The Book of Firsts

The earliest rabbis taught that each encounter with nature presents an opportunity for a blessing. In the most classical and fundamental of all Jewish legal texts, the *Mishnah* (ca. 200 C.E.) and the *Talmud* (ca. 500 C.E), these rabbis recommended that specific blessings ought to be recited upon seeing, for instance, a rainbow or lightning, or upon hearing thunder, or upon smelling fragrant herbs, flowers, trees, or fruits.

In this way, I suppose, the rabbis wished to use blessings as a spiritual exercise to heighten our sensory awareness of the sacredness of nature. As the great contemporary rabbinic sage Abraham Joshua Heschel said some decades ago, quoting from Isaiah: "'Lift up your eyes on high and see [who created these]' (Isa. 40:26). There is a higher form of seeing. We must learn how to lift up our eyes on high in order to see that the world is more a question than an answer . . . The grandeur of nature is only the beginning. Beyond the grandeur is God."[3]

PREPARATION

Creating a "Book of Firsts" is not actually one exercise. It is a series of exercises a child works at for many months or even many years. All you need to create this book is an empty notebook and a writing instrument. Your children might want to decorate or illustrate the cover, or they might not. No matter; what is important is what your children do with the book.

INSTRUCTIONS

Ask your children to keep the book handy whenever they are venturing outside. As they encounter the first flower poking up through the thawing earth in early springtime, or see the first firefly of the season, or smell the fragrance of the first grass cuttings of spring, or hear the sound of a newborn puppy, or feel the first winter snowflake on their noses, or any natural phenomenon they perceive as a "first," ask them to record the experience in their "Book of Firsts." Record the date and site of the experience, as well. You might also ask them to draw what they saw, heard, felt, or smelled next to their written entry. As a matter of fact, very young children can participate in this exercise simply by drawing what they experienced. They need not write about it. However, if they have something they wish to say, ask them to tell you, and you can write it down for them. Also record the date and site for them.

Then, I recommend that you ask your children to do some reflection and write or draw what they felt when they experienced this "first." This is difficult and may take some discussion with you or some quiet time alone.

Some children may not wish to reflect at all. This has happened to me when I have guided children through this exercise, but it is my experience that in their own time they will try. However, if your children do not wish to do any writing or reflecting, then honor that and let them go on to other things. For those children who do write or draw, let them know that anything they do is great; do encourage them, however, to describe if they felt happy, good, excited, surprised, or even frightened. (Sometimes young children find their encounters with some natural phenomena to be scary, at first. If so, help them to express these reactions, too.)

As they progress with this extended exercise, help them apprehend any bodily sensations that accompanied the emotions they expressed: When you felt excited, did you feel tingly? Warm? Where in your body did you feel these sensations? Any time we can enable our children to grow more in touch with their bodies and experience the somatic sense of their emotions, we have enriched their lives. Isn't that why we call emotional reactions "feelings"?

No Two Leaves Are Exactly Alike

In his tender fable, *The Friendly Snowflake*, about a young girl's journey into spiritual curiosity and discovery, M. Scott Peck introduces us to Jenny. Jenny learns that although each snowflake is unique, it belongs to a larger group that she thinks of as a family. She is convinced that one particular snowflake that she names Harry—and why not Harry?—is unique, and yet he belongs to a larger family of snowflakes. Harry and his "relatives" share many characteristics of "snowflakeness," yet he is different from all the rest—a point that even her older brother Dennis does not dispute. Peck's fable underscores one of the wonderful observations about our natural world: We might categorize different flora and fauna into groupings called *genera, phyla,* or *families;* yet upon closer scrutiny, despite the similarities that facilitate categorizations, we apprehend the mysterious and inimitable diversity that is nature.

Although my son Ilan is not a snowflake, he is most certainly unique. He was born into our family only sixteen days ago and has already exhibited what my wife Bari and I consider his "Ilanness." His sleep habits are much different from his older sister's at the same age, and you can only imagine at what time of day I am writing this. His nose and eyes (when open) are different from his sister Mikki's, and they seem to resemble either mine or Bari's, but not exactly. We expect that as Ilan grows through the years, he will grace us with as much "Ilannness" as we support and are open to discover, just as his sister has graced us with "Mikkiness."

Jewish folk wisdom has a saying: Each child brings his/her own blessing into the world. Perhaps most folk who were not privy to the esoteric speculation and practices of Jewish mysticism, *kabbala*, intuitively knew what Jewish mystics taught: Each one of us brings something utterly unique into our world, something no one else does. Jewish mystics called this a person's *tikkun*. Although in modern Hebrew it has a different connotation altogether, earlier mystics taught that one's *tikkun* was the individual gift each person carried within his/her soul that, when actualized, brought that person a true sense of bliss and harmony, and helped to move the cosmos toward greater and ultimate wholeness. I have always taken this to mean that each of us helps to complete the puzzle we call Creation when we are truly ourselves and actualize whatever it is within us that is our unique gift to ourselves, to others, to the world, and indeed, to the cosmos. When we seek to imitate others and ignore our own special gift, we only succeed in bringing redundancy to the world. No puzzle can be completed with a surplus of duplicate parts and a dearth of other pieces. Each of us is a vital piece of the puzzle called Creation. When we are sufficiently supported, encouraged, and given the necessary tools to discover for ourselves what our *tikkun* may be—in other words, who we really are—then we realize the self-actualization about which the psychologist Abraham Maslow spoke.

Author Polly Berrien Berends, in her book *Whole Child/Whole Parent,* reminds us that in addition to the many ways we can help our children grow spiritually, we parents, grandparents, teachers, clergy, and youthworkers can also become "beholders." Berends explains that "insofar as we behold our children as being beings rather than our own more or less pretty reflections and more or less talented creations, it becomes evident that each child is both uniquely beautiful and gifted. The essential spiritual goodness of the child is constantly kept in the forefront of our thoughts. Smiling to them readily, presenting them with beauty often, we assume, recognize, honor, and welcome forth this goodness, allowing it to take whatever surprising, unique, and beautiful shape it surely will."[4] As beholders we help each child discover his/her own *tikkun*.

Most certainly there are times to join with others in the service of our loved ones, of those in need, or of the flora, fauna, and environment of our planet. Just as certainly there are times to discover our individuality. We have a chance to teach our children how to make a difference both as part of a larger group and as unique individuals. The exercise that follows gives children a chance to discover that although there may be many representatives of a common grouping, each individual representative is unique. As Jenny discovered in Peck's fable, it is possible to be unique and still be part of a family.

PREPARATION

Have available several pieces of inexpensive white fabric for each child (10″ x 18″ or any approximation to this size is fine), a large assortment of regular crayons and fabric crayons, a magnifying glass or two or three, inked stamp pads in several different colors, a big piece of white paper large enough for the collective fingerprints of all participants, rubbing alcohol, and paper towels to clean the inky fingers.

One of your follow-up activities might involve sharing a story. For older children, *The Friendly Snowflake* is a good choice, and for younger children I recommend a book like *People*. You can find both of these books in the storytelling resource list at the back of the book. It has been my experience that despite the recommended target age of readers, some younger primary grade children enjoy Peck's *The Friendly Snowflake*, while some older children derive a great deal from Peter Spier's *People*. My advice is to obtain both books, and let your children give you their opinions. Also remember that your local bookstores and libraries might have other stories about discovering one's uniqueness and gracing our world with that special, particular gift.

You might also choose to use this exercise as an opportunity to express to your children that each is special and to speak about the unique traits or capabilities you see in each of them.

In late spring, summer, or early autumn, while the leaves are mature but not yet too brittle, invite your children to gather as many leaves as they can from bushes and plants, from low tree branches, and from the ground, in about fifteen minutes. Please make sure that any child who needs supervision and/or assistance is accompanied by an adult or an older child and request that they take care not to traumatize or injure any plant or tree as they collect their leaves. If they have a choice between selecting a leaf that has fallen to the ground and plucking one from a stem, encourage them to find a fresh leaf from the ground. At the end of about fifteen minutes, call them back to you.

Give each child an assortment of crayons and a couple of pieces of fabric. Ask them to place one leaf at a time (from their collections) under the fabric, and then ask them to use the crayon and rub over the leaf to create an imprint on the top surface of the fabric. Invite them to be as creative as they like. Perhaps they might place one leaf under this side of the fabric and rub over it in blue. Then they might put another kind of leaf under the other side of the fabric and rub over it with red. Or, maybe they will group many of the leaves next to one another right under the middle of the fabric and use only one color for the rubbing. It is up to them. Try to anticipate that younger children might need help placing some of their leaves under the fabric and learning how to rub over them. I will bet that with even the youngest children you will only have to show them how to do this once or twice before they are off creating leaf rubbings of their own.

After you sense that enough leaf rubbings have been done, ask your children questions like these: What do you notice that seems the same about all of the leaves you rubbed? What parts of these leaves are alike? Is there anything that seems to make one leaf look different from another? Are there leaves of different sizes? Are any of the shapes different? How are the shapes different?

Then, using the magnifying glasses, help the children make really close investigations of the leaves themselves. Under the magnifying glasses, what appears to make one leaf different from another? Explore the leaves, their similarities and their differences, for several minutes.

Point out, in the way most appropriate to their ages, that we call all of

76

these parts of nature that we collected, leaves. In some ways they resemble one another. In still other ways each is unique.

Now take out your ink pads. Give each child a chance to choose a particular pad and to use it to make his/her own fingerprint in one spot on the large piece of white paper. Keep all of the children's fingerprints fairly close together for the sake of observation and comparison. Here are some questions you might want to ask with and without the magnifying glasses: What do the fingerprints look like? Describe what fingerprints look like. What things do all fingerprints have in common? What makes your fingerprint look different from the others?

Now ask each child to write his/her name next to his/her fingerprint, and write the names of those who cannot do so for themselves. Ask each child to think of one thing that makes him or her special. Try to make it a word or two, or no more than a very brief sentence. Write it underneath or next to that child's name. Point out to your children that just as each fingerprint is different, each child is special and unique.

Using the follow-up activities I suggested or any other similar activity you would like, bring this exercise to a conclusion. Help your children make these observations in the manner best for them: In some ways leaves share similar characteristics, as do people, so we classify them with common labels like "leaves" or "children" or "people" or "human beings." In some ways members of leaf families/groupings and children families/groupings are different. In some ways our differences help us learn lessons about tolerance and diversity. In some ways our own individual uniqueness helps us to wonder about how we can use what is special about us to serve others and our planet.

Rather than use this exercise once and then put it away, hang the leaf rubbings and fingerprints around the house or classroom and use them to remind your children, from time to time, that they are special.

The Spiritual Scavenger Hunt

Do you remember going on scavenger hunts? Children love them; most likely you did, too, when you were younger. Perhaps the setting was camp, or school, or the old neighborhood. Maybe you were lucky enough to go on scavenger hunts in and around your own home. In addition to being great fun, scavenger hunts help our children meet the world in all of its variety and manifestations.

Helen Keller, who could neither see nor hear, opened her heart to the wonders of nature, and they entered her soul through that portal. "What a joy it is," she exclaimed, "to feel the soft, springy earth under my feet once more, to follow the grassy roads that lead to ferny brooks where I can bathe my fingers in a cataract of rippling notes."[5]

Any one of our senses, if attuned to the wonder-filled world, can perceive the marvels in the mundanity of our daily environments. The following exercise is designed to give our children a chance to encounter nature through all of their senses. It may seem like a simple game, but it is more than a game. It is an opportunity for our children to meet their world as if for the first time. Along the way, they will be guided by the voices of many extraordinary people who have shared with humanity the natural wonders they beheld with their hearts.

PREPARATION

After a preparatory exercise, gather your children together. You might want to divide a large group into smaller groups, or you might wish to form pairs, or you might invite each child to participate on his/her own. You might even decide to gather everyone into one group and participate with them yourself. It is your choice. Certainly, make sure that the area of exploration is safe and that young children have adequate supervision and assistance.

Give each participant a list of items for which to search and a pencil. The list is printed below. Those children who cannot read ought to be placed with an older child or adult who can. The objective is to roam the designated field area until each item on the list has been found and collected in the bag provided for each group/pair/individual.

INSTRUCTIONS

Read each item and follow its directions; here is the list:

1. Ralph Waldo Emerson once wrote that "the earth laughs in flowers." Imagine that every time the earth laughed a new flower appeared. Look

around you and see the flowers. The earth must be filled with laughter. Go find a flower and put it in your bag.

2. Walt Whitman said, "Now I see the secret of the making of the best persons. It is to grow in the open air, and to eat and sleep with the earth." Take a nice deep breath of the fresh air. Now list five foods that come from the earth:

_____

_____

After you have finished, find some soil that gives birth to the foods you eat, and put some in your bag.

3. Kahlil Gibran asked us to "forget not that the earth delights to feel your bare feet and the winds long to play with your hair." Stop for a moment and close your eyes. Feel the touch of the wind on your face. Feel it blow through your hair. Can you hear the wind? Does it make a sound? Now open your eyes and find something the wind can blow around and place it in your bag.

4. A Native American proverb teaches us that "the frog does not drink up the pond in which he lives." Of course the frog does not drink up all the water in the pond where he lives. If he did, where would he live? It would be silly for a frog to destroy the place where he lives. Yet we all live in a place called "The Earth," and sometimes we do things that ruin it and hurt it. Look around you. Are there any signs of pollution or graffiti? Don't these ruin and hurt our world? Name five things we can do to keep our world beautiful and healthy:

_____

_____

_____

_____

5. Henry David Thoreau wrote, "The birds I heard today . . . sang as freshly as if it had been the first morning of creation." Stop for just a moment. Stand completely still and silent. Can you hear a bird singing? Listen. Can you hear its song? Now look around you and find something that a bird would use to make a nest. Put that item in your bag.

6. At the beginning of the Bible, we read, "And God said, 'Let the earth sprout vegetation: seed-bearing plants, fruit trees of every kind on earth that bear fruit with the seed in it.' And it was so. The earth brought forth vegetation: seed-bearing plants of every kind and trees of every kind

bearing fruit with the seed in it. And God saw that this was good."(Gen. 1:11–12) Take a good look around you. Find three natural things that you think are good and place them in your bag.

7. Crowfoot asked us to think about this: "What is life? It is the flash of a firefly in the night. It is the breath of a buffalo in the winter. It is the little shadow which runs across the grass and loses itself in the Sunset." The North American Indians have always considered the earth to be sacred. Go to the dictionary and look up the word *sacred*. (If there are children who do not know how to use a dictionary, look up the word for them and explain it.) Write down what it means in your own words:

_____

_____

8. Stop for a moment and listen to the sounds of our world. Name three sounds you hear:

_____

_____

_____

9. Look around you and name something that is blue, something that is brown, something that is green, and something that is yellow:

_____

_____

_____

10. Find something that is rough, something that is smooth, something that is soft, something that is hard, and put these four things in your bag after you list them here:

_____

_____

_____

Of course, you may feel free to add to these items, rewrite them, or substitute your own. No one loses in this exercise. Everyone who participates wins. When all of the children have finished, gather everyone together and let them show and tell about what they have found, and invite them to discuss their responses to some of the questions.

Climbing the Ladder: An Imaginal Journey [6]

I have called this an imaginal journey and not a visualization because visualization is used by some to refer exclusively to sight—the act of seeing. On the other hand, I believe that the term *imaginal* includes the possibility of employing more than merely the sense of sight.

PREPARATION

If you do this exercise indoors, I invite you to cleanse the room with incense or diffused essential oils about one-half hour before doing the exercise. Consider playing the music recommended by Campbell for passive imagery. This exercise can also be done outside. Wherever you choose, find a comfortable spot for your children to sit. They may need soft mats or blankets. If you are outside, try not to sit directly under the sun if it is a warm day. If you are inside, try to eliminate all sources of external noise and interruption. Read through the script. If you wish to make changes that seem more helpful for your children, please do so. This is a comparatively long exercise. As I recommended when presenting Joseph Cornell's "Tree Imagery," you may want to abbreviate the script. However, I have found that children as young as five and six have enjoyed it all the way through. Yet, you know your children best. Emend the length and language to meet your children's needs.

As always, if your children are uncomfortable closing their eyes, I have some options for you: First, you may wish to select another exercise that does not invite them to keep their eyes closed for as long a period of time. Second, you may invite your children to close their eyes long enough to listen quietly to some of the music and try one of the brief breathing exercises. Third, you might invite them to keep their eyes closed for as long as they choose during the exercise and permit them to open their eyes when they grow uncomfortable. Fourth, it is also possible for them to sit quietly with their eyes open and listen to the script as if it were a story. That has happened during some of my workshops, and the children have really enjoyed "the nice story." If it is at all possible, however, I recommend that this exercise be done with the children's eyes closed.

Finally, before you begin, quiet the children with some music, a purification ritual, and/or a breathing exercise.

Sit comfortably. Relax. Close your eyes. Breathe deeply and slowly for a while, in through your nose and out through your mouth. After a while, begin to make your out breath longer and lazier through your mouth than your inhalation: Breathe in normally through your nose, and breathe out slowly through your mouth. Breathe in normally through your nose, and let your breath flow out of your mouth very slowly.

Now with your eyes still closed, breathe normally and imagine that you are in the midst of the most beautiful park you have ever seen. See and smell the trees and flowers. Feel the warm summer sun on your head, your neck, and your shoulders. Hear the breeze as it blows through the leafy, tree branches, and feel it as it refreshes you and cools you just a bit.

Look around for a moment. Imagine all there is in this wonderful place. Feel how calm and peaceful you are.

The fresh, flower-scented air fills your nostrils and floats down to your lungs. Then out it comes, returning along the same path it used to enter just a moment before. In and out, in and out, in and out.

Have you ever really noticed your breathing before? So this is what brings life to your body! How simple! How miraculous!

Now imagine all of the beauty that surrounds you in this park. Imagine the many different kinds of flowers, many-hued in color. Smell the fragrance of the grass and the trees, the flowers and the plants. Hear the birds sing, the bees drone, the leaves rustle in the breeze. Take a moment to see, smell, and hear life in this park. . . .

Imagine turning around and finding a ladder standing in front of you. Its feet are planted firmly in the ground while its uppermost rungs reach through the clouds and into the heavens above.

You are curious, so you approach the ladder to examine it more closely. When you try to shake it, you discover that it stands firmly, and no matter how hard you try, you cannot shake it. Steady and straight it rises into the sky, and you grow curious about the worlds above. So you begin to climb rung by rung, step by step, slowly at first, until you get used to the journey and confident about your ability to make it to the top.

Each step brings you higher, but you are not frightened. In fact, it feels great to climb high into the deep blue sky. You grow stronger with every step. Below you is the park. You can imagine it so far below you.

Up into the fluffy, white clouds you go. Notice how it feels to climb through them.

Now, upward you climb. Higher and higher. Only the bright blue sky and the glowing yellow sun stretch above you. Surrounded by the golden blue light of the heavens, you feel safe and protected. It seems as though that golden blue light illumines you with its glow. Your skin reflects its radiance and glows like the sky. At this height, your whole body glows with that golden blue light. You shine like the heavens. It makes you feel so alive, so filled with energy, confidence, and joy.

The sky glows with golden blue light, and you glow, too. From your inside to your outside, you glow. Your glow melts into the glow of the heavens until you realize that you are part of the heavens, and the heavens are part of you. It is like you are part of the sky. You have never felt so wonderful. So enjoy this great feeling. Take all the time you want. (Pause for a moment.)

It is time to return down the ladder. Climb down from the heavens filled with joy, filled with warmth, filled with well-being, filled with wonder and amazement. You know that you can return to this place anytime you wish. You know that the power to climb the ladder is within you. The power is yours. You can call upon this power whenever you choose.

Down the ladder you go. Step by step you count as you descend: one step . . . two . . . three . . . four . . . five . . . six . . . seven . . . eight . . . nine . . . and ten. You have reached the ground once more. Above you the ladder stretches up into the sky, all the way to the highest heavens. But you have returned to earth. You can hear all of the familiar sounds around you. Listen for sounds that you recognize. . . . You know exactly where you are. You can feel the ground where you are seated. . . . You can feel your toes and your legs. . . . You can feel yourself breathing in and out. . . . When you are ready, you can open your eyes.

(When the children have their eyes open, continue with the end of the exercise.) Your journey is over for now. And the good news is that you can go back whenever you want. You have that power. You have that choice. You are a very important part of the universe.

The Blossoming Rose

I want to end this Part with an exercise that includes something from the natural world that might be a gift for our children to carry with them wherever they go. Especially in their early years, our children are blossoming. They are unfolding, granting us glimpses of their potentials and unique gifts. For a while, they will be in our homes or classrooms, cared for and nourished by us. Eventually, however, they will go out on their own. Hopefully, we will have helped them discover their own resourcefulness, their sense of who they are and who they are becoming, and their fortitude and truth within.

In this Part I have offered you exercises which will help ground your children in the wonder and wisdom of the natural world. Perhaps we might also have guided them to their own understandings of the value of stillness, observation, and awareness. With this concluding exercise, it is my hope that a simple creation of the universe, like a rose, will furnish an imaginal resource upon which they can draw when they need strength, a reminder of their developing potentials and an appreciation of their own unique sacredness.

Aside from being a flower that enjoys almost universal appreciation for its beauty and fragrance, historically the rose has been a powerful religious and mythic symbol. Throughout time, it has symbolized perfection to some, eternity, fertility, and life to others, and the passion and mystery of life to still others.[7] Of all the roses that exist, this exercise focuses upon a white rose, the "flower of light," because of its connotation of spiritual unfolding.[8]

The rose's innate power to convey and facilitate the process of unfolding has been recognized by poets, educators, holistic healers, and psychologists in our own time. For example, we know that the Italian psychiatrist Roberto Assagioli used just such an image to help convey the unfolding process of the psyche;[9] and aromatherapists have known for a long time that the scent of a rose has therapeutic effects that aid the natural emergence of our true selves by inducing relaxation and dispelling depression, anxiety, and grief.

What power embodied in such a beautiful natural package! This exercise is intended to implant the blessings of the rose in the hearts of our blossoming children.

PREPARATION

As with the preceding imaginal journey, if you do this exercise indoors, I invite you to cleanse the room with incense or diffused essential oils about one-half hour before doing the exercise. Again, contemplate the use of music recommended by Campbell for passive imagery. This exercise, too, can be done inside or outside. Wherever you choose, find a comfortable spot for your children to sit. Provide them with soft mats or blankets if they are requested or desired. If you are outside, try not to sit directly under the sun if it is a warm day. If you are inside, try to eliminate all sources of external noise and interruption. Read through the script, as I have recommended with every script in this book. Feel free to make any changes that are better for your children. You might want to place a rosebud and a blossomed rose in front of your children, or simply leave the imaging of the rose up to them without any external aid or focus.

If your children are uncomfortable closing their eyes, review the options I have offered you previously: selecting another exercise that does not invite them to keep their eyes closed for as long a period of time; inviting your children to close their eyes long enough to listen quietly to some of the music and try one of the brief breathing exercises; permitting them to keep their eyes closed for as long as they choose and to open their eyes when they grow uncomfortable; or allowing them to sit quietly with their eyes open and listen to the script as if it were a story. If it is at all possible, however, I always recommend that exercises like this one and the previous one be done with your children's eyes closed. If that is not possible for your children, honor their feelings and try one of my suggestions.

Finally, I believe that it enhances this exercise to quiet your children first with some music, a purification ritual, and/or a breathing exercise.

INSTRUCTIONS

Sit comfortably. Relax. Close your eyes. Breathe deeply and slowly for a while; in through your nose, and out through your mouth. After a while, begin to make your out breath longer and lazier through your mouth than your inhalation: Breathe in normally through your nose, and breathe out slowly through your mouth. Breathe in normally through your nose, and let your breath flow out of your mouth very slowly.

Now feel the beating of your heart. In the silence of this moment, notice your heart beating. If you cannot feel your heart beating, place your hand over your chest. Count with it as it beats . . . one . . . two . . . three. . . . Count with it up to ten beats as you sit still and calm.

Imagine your heart as it beats, and imagine that every time it beats it opens up more and more. Imagine that inside your heart, a white rose is growing. It was first a seed, and now it is a young rosebud ready to blossom. The more your heart beats, the more your heart opens, the more the white rose becomes visible. You can see it. It is so pure, so young, still a rosebud ready to blossom. Its petals are closed tightly at first. Yet with every beat of your heart, the petals begin to open, the bud begins to blossom, the white rose begins to unfold. Imagine this beautiful, white rosebud unfolding inside your own heart. Keep imagining it until it has opened fully. What a magnificent white rose radiating a pure, bright white light! The rose shines in a brilliant, sparkling white light. Rays of this light spread from your heart to your whole chest which is now filled with this sparkling clean, pure, powerful white light. You can feel the power. Now your whole chest is filled with this white light, and you can feel how happy that makes you. Now the white light from the rose spreads until your arms and legs, your chest and stomach are filled by its radiance. Your whole body is beaming with this pure white light. It shines through your hands, your feet, your head, until you are surrounded by a beautiful white bubble which grew from the special white rose which grew from your heart. Imagine that you are surrounded by a glow of white light that makes you feel warm, safe, and so very happy. (Pause for a moment to allow your children to stay here with this particular image.)

While you are surrounded by this white light, you are always safe, you are always okay, you are filled with love, and you feel loved. You have another moment to stay in your white, glowing bubble, and then it will be time to let the rose return inside your heart. (Pause for a brief moment.)

Feel the beat of your heart again. Feel it as it beats . . . one . . . two . . . three. With each beat, your rose closes just a little bit more. Its light fades. The petals begin to close. Soon, the white rose is a rosebud again. Slowly, with every beat of your heart, it returns to its safe place inside your heart. Slowly, with every beat, imagine your heart closing. Slowly, let your image of the rosebud go. Allow the rosebud to return to your heart. Let it stay there until you need it or want it again.

Feel your heart beating. If you need to, place your hand over your heart and feel it beating. Feel the strong, consistent, healthy beat of your heart. The rose is always there. That love, that safety, that health, that protection, that special power is always there. Whenever you need your rose, just take a visit inside. It is there. It will always be there, even when you are sad, even when you are mad, even when you are disappointed, and especially when you are most happy and feeling most loved.

Now it is time to return to where we are sitting, to this day, to this hour, to this minute. It is time to return to everyone who is with you. You know exactly where you are. You can feel the ground where you are seated. . . . You can feel your toes and your legs. . . . You can feel yourself breathing in and out. . . . Take a few full, slow breaths. Notice how you feel. When you are ready, you can open your eyes.

(When the children have their eyes open, continue with the end of the exercise.) You can make your rose blossom whenever you want. That power is yours, and it will always be yours.

87

NOTES

1. Joseph Bharat Cornell, "How to Be an Effective Nature Guide (A Few Suggestions for Good Teaching)," in *Spiritual Parenting in the New Age*, ed. Anne Carson (Freedom, CA: The Crossing Press, 1989), pp. 181–83.

2. Midrash is a genre of Jewish literature through which its authors seek to probe, examine, interpret, and extend the Biblical text. One type of midrashic literature is legal, and one is lore. There are many classical and medieval works subsumed under the category of midrash. Rabbis and others who wish to delve into the Biblical text for meaning, value, vision, and insight, continue to create literature of this midrashic genre even today. Often midrashic literature included other literary forms like parables, fables, and legends. Some of the best-loved and most popular teaching tales in Jewish tradition are derived from midrashic literature.

3. Abraham Joshua Heschel, *God in Search of Man: A Philosophy of Judaism* (New York: Farrar, Straus and Giroux, 1958), p. 97.

4. Polly Berrien Berends, *Whole Child/Whole Parent*, rev. ed. (New York: Harper & Row Publishers, 1987), pp. 252–53.

5. Steven Van Matre and Bill Weiler, eds., *The Earth Speaks: An Acclimitization Journal* (Warrenville, IL: The Institute for Earth Education, 1983), p. 30.

6. This imaginal journey is adapted from a story in a new book of mine, entitled *The Twenty-Two Gates to the Garden*, that will be published in the summer of 1994 by Jason Aronson, Inc. It is a collection of twenty-two mystical tales based upon age-old spiritual wisdom.

7. J. C. Cooper, *An Illustrated Encyclopedia of Traditional Symbols* (London: Thames and Hudson, 1978), p. 141.

8. Cooper, p. 141.

9. Piero Ferrucci, *What We May Be: Techniques for Psychological and Spiritual Growth Through Psychosynthesis* (Los Angeles: Jeremy P. Tarcher, 1982), p. 132.

Part Three

Going Inside

Children and Meditation

Meditation comes from the Sanskrit word *medha* and means "wisdom." Not all of the wisdom our children gain in a lifetime needs to come from external authorities and popular experts. It seems that we adults have come to depend so much on others to tell us what to do or what to believe that authority connotes something given to us from outside ourselves. It does not have to be that way for our children. We can help our children discover a great gift by guiding them to recognize and believe in their own inherent wisdom. In the stillness of any given moment, when the turbulence of their worlds has grown calm, our children will come to perceive their own valuable insights, and with our support, they will gain confidence in themselves. They will come to trust their own intuition. Thus, they will contribute their own light to our world rather than merely mirroring another's.

Meditation has been practiced by people of every place and time since the dawn of humanity. Jews have practiced what they call *kavannah*, while Hindus have practiced *japa*, Sufis have practiced *zikr*, Tibetan Buddhists have practiced *shamata* and *vipassana*, and Zen masters have practiced *zazen*.[1] Among experienced teachers or practitioners of meditation, there are as many opinions about what meditation is as there are names for it. For some, meditation is a path to a stillness of mind and body, and for others it is a path to God or enlightenment. The word itself means wisdom, so it might fairly be said that meditation is a path to wisdom. Whether that wisdom comes from communion with what some call God or others call the Buddha Nature, or whether it comes from a quiet moment of living is a matter of particularity and personal orientation.

Traditionally, the range of tools to aid the aspirant is as varied as are the definitions and names. Some have found their paths through the use of: mantras; foci of concentration like candles, breathing, or mandalas; mind puzzles like Zen *koans* that discourage us from relying upon our logic; chants or walks; performance of mundane activities; or even high-tech audiotapes that employ barely audible music or chants vibrating at the frequencies of *alpha, beta, theta,* or *delta* sound waves.

I based my choice of exercises that I call meditations in this book upon my personal experience with children. I have witnessed them help children grow still, more attuned to the moment, more conscious of the simple wonders that surround them daily, and more able to quiet their minds and bodies. I believe that Thich Nhat Hanh would call these characteristics of *mindfulness.* I have found that meditation is a path to mindful living, and these exercises are tools. If you wish to go further or survey the varied teachings of recent and contemporary masters, I suggest you peruse the resources I have listed at the back of this book.

Like all of the exercises included here, the meditation exercises can be enjoyed by children young and old. Even children as young as three and four can do a simple breathing exercise and be asked to notice their breath going in and their breath going out. In my opinion, concentrating on that most basic activity for ten to fifteen seconds constitutes a meditation.

The Buddhist master Rev. Jiyu Kennett Roshi notes that "in the east the average child is taught to meditate as soon as it is possible for it to sit upright; i.e., around one or two years old. No doctrine is put into the child's head. The mother and father, and the rest of the family, will sit quietly in front of the family altar; the child without being restrained, will either sit on the floor for a few moments or roll around on the floor with the parents taking no notice . . . In a very short time the child wants to sit like the parents . . ."[2] Indeed, she recalls seeing "children at the age of two and a half doing formal meditation in the laymen's meditation hall in Sojiji—and doing a wonderful job. I have photographs of them. These children do a meditation so pure and exquisite it is unbelievable to watch; but they would not be able to discuss the Buddha Nature with you. . . ."[3]

If you are attempting to introduce very young children to meditation, you would do well to heed Kennett's advice and simply allow them to be with you as you meditate. You might also try placing the very youngest children upon your lap and rubbing their backs gently or giving them a small ball of clay to hold.[4] A short time—fifteen seconds, thirty seconds, a minute or more—is fine for the beginning. If this ritual becomes a part of their lives, young children will come to respect and value meditation, and they will grow to sit for longer and longer periods of time.

Older children might be introduced to meditation in a similar manner. Those who seem uncomfortable with any of the exercises can be invited to sit along side you and observe silently. Even if they are not participating in the exercises, requesting that they be respectful to you and others will help inculcate a sense of respect for meditation itself. Share with your children what you derive from meditation.

I recommend experimenting with music, with lighting, and with different preparatory exercises. For some children, breathing exercises alone can be wonderful meditations. Other children like to do a series of yoga postures before meditation. Still others prefer to use some incense, tranquil lighting, and a bit of relaxing music before engaging in sitting forms of meditation.

93

ADDITIONAL ADVICE

1. For sitting meditations, it is good for children to sit comfortably upright and cross-legged, if not in half-lotus posture (left foot placed on the right thigh or the right foot placed on the left thigh) or full-lotus posture (left foot placed on the right thigh and the right foot placed on the left thigh). Lying down tends to promote sleepiness. Ask them to try to keep their spines as straight as possible. Help them find a position that takes very little effort to maintain. The last thing you want is for them to be so uncomfortable as to be distracted by their discomfort.

2. Children might try to place a cushion under the very edge of their hips/buttocks to keep their spines erect in a more comfortable manner.

3. Those who cannot be comfortable sitting unsupported upon the ground or upon pillows may sit in a straight-backed chair or up against a wall.

4. Help them find a comfortable way to hold their hands. They might try placing one open hand upon the opposite palm or laying them open upon their knees either palms up or palms down.

5. No matter what kind of meditation they are doing, it is best neither to be famished nor to have just finished eating. They will not be able to turn their attention away from their stomachs if they are too full or too empty, and they might feel sleepy if they meditate after a big meal.

6. If the meditation invites them to focus upon some object or words, do not let them worry if their minds wander. Allow them to note that they have drifted and to acknowledge and honor the images and thoughts that have entered their consciousness; then invite them to return to the focus of their attention.

7. Try to turn off sources of external noise or interruption like radios, televisions, stereos, and phones.

8. Ask them to keep their breathing even, natural, and relaxed.

As we have seen, there are as many schools of meditation as there are great teachers. My own survey of the literature leads me to recommend that you experiment with as many kinds of meditation as you like, using the resources I have provided. Make your own choice about how you and your family or students begin to meditate. However, I think that the following three meditation exercises are as good a place as any to begin a practice of meditation with your children. These scripted exercises were created by a leader among those who teach meditation and creative fantasy to children, Deborah Rozman. Although Rozman targets specific age groups for the first two meditations, you know your children best. Use these exercises and adapt them according to your instincts about your own children or students. For instance, you might find that your two-year-old is capable of enjoying the first meditation or that your fifteen-year-old looks forward to the second. When it comes to your children, you are the expert who counts most.

Inside Exercises

A Meditation Exercise for
Three- to Five-Year-Olds

PREPARATION

These meditations can be done inside or outside. It is important, however, that you choose a site where you will not suffer any interruptions. Try to select a place that is clean, free of too much dust, malodorous scents, strong sun, or gusts of wind. Your children might be more comfortable if they each have a blanket or exercise mat upon which to sit. There are some meditation teachers who recommend a small cushion placed either between their knees, if they are sitting on bent legs, or for the edge of their buttocks to keep their spines as erect as possible. The great masters advise students not to meditate on a full stomach or a noticeably empty stomach. Dress in light, comfortable clothing.

Before continuing with these or any of the other meditations in this Part, you might wish to review my general comments and recommendations in Part One.

Sit up straight with your legs crossed and your hands palms up on your knees or thighs. Be sure to keep your back straight. Have you ever seen puppets on strings? Imagine there's a string on top of your head pulling you up so your spine is straight. Close your eyes. Now breathe in through your nose slowly. Keep your mouth closed. Breathe out through your nose. . . . Let's do this again. Breathe in as I count to three: 1 . . . 2 . . . 3 . . . . Hold to three: 1 . . . 2 . . . 3 . . . . Breathe out slowly through the nose to a count of three: 1 . . . 2 . . . 3 . . . . Let's do this again and again. (Repeat the 1 . . . 2 . . . 3 . . . breathing three or four times.) Now just relax and breathe like you usually do. Be still. In . . . and . . . out . . . in . . . and . . . out. . . . Feel like you are a wave on the sea. Rising slowly . . . up . . . and . . . down . . . each time you breathe . . . in . . . and . . . out. . . . Feel like you are the sea. . . . (Rest quietly, everyone being the sea until the children start to move or be restless.)

(Then say): Now let's tense your whole body, make fists, tense all the muscles in your legs, feet, arms, chest, and don't forget your face. Tense your mouth and nose, too. Now, still sitting up straight, let go. Let all the energy out, out, out until you are empty, relaxed, completely empty. Not a drop left. Now, still sitting up straight, (whisper) very quietly, we look inside our self behind our closed eyes. Look at a place right between your eyebrows inside your forehead. Look up a little, and look inward. Feel like you are at the center of your Self, deep in your heart. There is a shining light right inside you, right there. Be the light.

Rozman notes that if the child is not quiet and relaxed after "being the sea," do the tensing and relaxing, and then add: Each time you breathe in and out like a wave, you will go deeper and deeper into meditation. I'll count waves, and when I get to ten, you will be a quiet wave, and you will be the calm sea, and you will be deeply relaxed. (Count slowly following the child's breathing.) 1 . . . 2 . . . 3 . . . 4 . . . 5 . . . 6 . . . 7 . . . 8 . . . 9 . . . 10. . . . There, you are the calm, quiet sea.

If the child continues to be very restless, Rozman suggests that you have him/her lie down on his/her back with legs and arms straight during the meditation. Yet there is a danger s/he may fall asleep. That is why it is preferable for him/her to learn how to meditate sitting up, if at all possible. In addition, Rozman recommends that very restless children be permitted to move their bodies and sway like the sea and the waves and gradually calm down to stillness.[5]

A Meditation Exercise for
Six- to Ten-Year-Olds

PREPARATION

Begin this exercise with the sea relaxation you used for the three- to five-year-olds.

INSTRUCTIONS

Now that you are quiet and relaxed and perfectly still, let us imagine that we're at the top of a tall building, and we're going to walk down the staircase to the ground floor. We are putting one foot down after the other, and it is a long staircase. We are going down, down, down, down, one step at a time. 1...2...3...4...5...6...7...8...9...10.... Now we turn the corner and go down another stairway. 1...2...3...4...5...6...7...8...9...10.... And now we keep going, one step after the other. 1...2...3...4...5...6...7...8...9...10.... And now we are at the bottom, and there's a trap door leading into our hearts. We open the door and walk inside our own hearts. *Listen*...to what your heart is telling you.... Ask it a question, to yourself, not out loud.... *Listen* for the answer. Be sure to ask your question.

(Pause before going on.) Now, very quietly feel your toes. Imagine that your toes are disappearing, vanishing into the air. Now, feel your feet. Feel them disappear into the light around...no feet, only light.... Feel your ankles and feel them vanish, disappear. Now your legs are vanishing. Feel your knees and feel them disappear, dissolve into atoms and energy. Imagine your buttocks and stomach disappear, dissolving into light. Imagine your buttocks and stomach disappear into light, dissolved into the air. Feel your chest and feel it totally disappear. And now the arms . . . they're so light they are disappearing. Feel your shoulders and feel them vanish into light. Feel your chin and feel it dissolve. . . . And now imagine your mouth and cheeks and nose dissolve into pure energy, into light. Your eyes and forehead are disappearing, and now the very top of your head has disappeared into light. . . . There is no body left, it has entirely disappeared.

All of its atoms have dissolved into pure energy . . . light . . . nothing. There is nothing left, just your real Self. Nothing left but your awareness . . . that came to earth when you were born, to live, to work, to play, and to grow in your body. But you had forgotten who you really are. You began to believe you were your body. Now do you remember what it's like to have no body? Who are you? Are you space? (This exercise can also be done lying down, before bedtime or, if the child is restless, during the meditation.)

Let's slowly remake our bodies now and imagine all our flesh and bones and blood and organs coming back to us. Let's imagine our senses returning. Our touch . . . we can feel our bones and muscles again. Our taste . . . we can sense the taste of our own mouth again. Our smell . . . we can smell our body, and we can smell the room. Our hearing . . . we can hear more and more sounds. We can hear our breathing, the voices are louder. What else can we hear? Now last of all our sight . . . let's open our eyes and look around. What's the first thing you see? Do things look different?

My experience has taught me that you may wish to use the questions asked at the end of the meditation as catalysts to conversation, or you may choose another way to bring closure to this exercise—simply let the experience stand for itself. Just let things be.

Five Senses Meditation

PREPARATION

Rozman suggests that before you begin this meditation, ask your children about the five senses. What are they? What do we use them for?

How do they teach us about the world? This script is a slight adaptation of the one in her book.

Sit up straight and comfortably. Breathe slowly and deeply. Now go into your Source, the Center within you. Close your eyes. Pretend you have never seen anything before. You have never seen color, people, sun, trees, anything. . . . Then close your ears with your fingers . . . bring all the sounds back into the Source. . . . Imagine all the energy in your nerves that you use to feel and touch with come back into the Source. . . . Now, imagine you can't smell anything. . . . and now imagine you can't taste anything . . . imagine that all of your senses have disappeared into the Source. Concentrate on the Source and make your very self disappear into the Source. . . . Life is rhythm, nature is rhythm, life and death, night and day, we breathe in and out, in and out. So, too, in meditation we bring all the energy from our five senses back into the Source, and then we let the energy flow out again into our senses which we need to use to live in the world. In and out. . . . Now, let's imagine our senses returning. . . . Our taste, we can sense the taste of our own mouths again. . . . Our smell, we can smell our bodies, and we can smell the room and other bodies. . . . Our touch, we can feel our bones and muscles again. . . . Our hearing, we can hear more and more sounds. . . . We can hear our breathing. What else can we hear? Listen. . . . Now last of all our sight. Let's open our eyes and look around. What is the first thing you see? Do things look different?

Again, the concluding questions might serve as the basis for conversation, for drawing, for writing in diaries and journals, or they might simply be allowed to linger in the souls of your children as seeds of mystery and wonder.

Body Awareness Meditation

The Jesuit priest and renowned storyteller Anthony de Mello believed that "far too many people live too much in their head . . . as a result they rarely live in the present."[6] Prayer and awareness evolve out of contact with the present. So to get children out of their heads, where contemporary education seems to keep them, and help them awaken to the present, de Mello recommended returning to our bodily senses.

PREPARATION

The next scripted exercise may be used to help your children get in touch with their bodies and, by doing so, live more in the present moment. Before trying this exercise, select a preparatory exercise that will help quiet all participants. Perhaps a few of the yoga postures or breathing exercises will help bring your children from their heads into their bodies. Try some of my recommendations for music or for incense. Keep in mind my discussion of meditation exercises for this exercise, too.

When your children have completed this exercise once, ask them to return to their breathing and start the exercise all over again. Over time, after they become accustomed to it, ask them to try to do the body scan two or three times. Spend only a couple of seconds visiting each part of the body, but do try to read the script slowly and softly. If you wish to visit other parts of the body, go right ahead. If you wish to find other questions to help you and your children explore all the various parts of your bodies, be my guest.

INSTRUCTIONS

Now, get comfortable. Relax. Settle into a seated position with your hands lying limply upon your thighs or knees, or lie upon your back with your hands at your sides and your legs spread apart slightly. Breathe in. Make it a slow, smooth breath. Breathe out. Make it slow and smooth. Breathe in again and feel your breath enter your nose and fill your belly. Feel your belly rise . . . and then fall. Do this several times. Breathe nicely and slowly. Now, I will ask you to visit different parts of your body in order to feel that part of your body. You will only spend a couple of seconds visiting each location. Start with your neck. What does it feel like? Now move to your right arm. What does it feel like? Is it heavy or light? Warm or cold? Now move to your left arm. What does it feel like? What do your fingers feel like? Now move to your chest. Feel your heart beat. Feel your lungs expand with each breath. Now move to your belly.

What does it feel like? Feel it rise with each breath and fall as you expel that breath. Now move to your right leg. What does it feel like? Is it heavy or light? Warm or cold? What do your clothes feel like against your skin? Now move to your left leg. What does it feel like? What do your clothes feel like against your skin? Now move to your right foot. What does it feel like? Can you feel your toes? Now move to your left foot. What does it feel like? Can you feel those toes?

(If your children are doing this scan two or more times consecutively, then add this last instruction only after they have completed their last scan and have just reached their toes.) Now breathe in and out once. Stay quiet, sitting comfortably with your eyes closed for a countdown of five . . . four . . . three . . . two . . . one. Open your eyes when you are ready.

Awakening to the World Outside Us

First a story: Once there was a diver who made his living collecting pearls from oysters. Each day he would dive into the depths of the bay and search for oysters that held the treasures he sought. Once he located an oyster, he would pry it open and compel it to release the gem it held within. However, one oyster had observed this diver for a long time. It noticed that he always searched for the pearls inside the oyster. He never looked in any other direction. So this oyster thought of a plan. It opened up and allowed its pearl to roll on to the rocky ledge on which it sat. The pearl was no longer inside this oyster, but it could not have been more than six inches away. According to his schedule, the diver submerged into the depths of the bay the next day. He swam and searched for oysters. He found one and then another. Each time, he swam straight for the marine mollusk and compelled it to release its pearl. Then he discovered the oyster that rested upon the rocky ledge. Of course, he set his eyes directly upon it and swam straight toward it without diversion. When he reached the ledge, he compelled the oyster to open, but he found nothing inside. Disgusted and surprised, he turned away and continued his search for other oysters. As he turned away, his leg brushed past the pearl that lay right in front of his very eyes. Yet he did not see it. He would never enjoy that treasure.

And so it is with those of us who are so focused we see only what we set our sights upon, attain only what we aim for, enjoy only what we expect. In his book *Visions of Innocence*, Edward Hoffman calls our attention to all of those people whose peak spiritual experiences occurred in the plainest sight possible; he called this category "Backyard Visions." Apparently, one does not have to travel to the Grand Canyon or to the Himalayas to be graced with spiritual experiences. Believe it or not, some of the most inspiring peak experiences Hoffman recorded involved ordinary backyard pond life, rose gardens, streams, everyday wind, sunlight, grassy lawns, lazy strolls, and glimpses from bedroom windows.

The rabbis asked the question: Why was Moses graced by God's revelation at a burning bush, a mundane mountain plant? After all, the God of all the universe, the Creator of all creation could have gotten Moses' attention with a thunderbolt, a shooting star, or a volcanic eruption. Their teaching: The leader of Israel was to be one who was able to recognize the sacred in the ordinary, the epiphany in the mundane.

The Dominican priest, theologian, and leading contemporary teacher of a creation-centered spirituality, Matthew Fox, speaks of creation as "original blessing."[7] Fox writes that "the universe loves us every day the sun rises, and the creator loves us through creation."[8] Such love can be shared with our children.

Our children deserve to be sanctified with this kind of "original blessing." But how? Perhaps we can help them become mindful of the wonders that sit right before their eyes, disguised in mundanity, like the oyster's pearl that lay before the diver. While the diver never discovered the treasure there before him, we can help our children develop this kind of mindfulness through the exercises in this book. The following is one that I have found to be most successful.

PREPARATION

Provide your children with comfortable blankets to sit upon if the grass in your backyard, or local park, or school grounds is wet or rocky. Choose one of the preparatory exercises that you have found to be quieting. I would also advise that you do this exercise after you have completed the previous exercise "Body Awareness Meditation." That exercise brings a mindfulness focused on the internal world, so it seems to be a perfect compliment to an exercise that promotes mindfulness of the external world. You can refer, as well, to some of the collections of nature writings and stories that I recommended earlier on pp. 57, 70–71, 87n–88n, or the marvelous anthology *The Earth Speaks,* edited by Steven Van Matre and Bill Weiler. These might furnish introductory or summary readings.

The following script has worked for me, but feel free to make any changes that seem more appropriate for your children.

INSTRUCTIONS

Now, get comfortable. Relax. Settle into a comfortable seated position. Breathe in. Make it a slow, smooth breath. Breathe out. Make it slow and smooth. Breathe in again and feel your breath enter your nose and fill your belly. Feel your belly rise . . . and then fall. Do this several times. Breathe nicely and slowly. In a moment you will place your hands over your ears and turn your head very, very slowly, all the way from one side to the other. Try to see every flower or plant, every insect, every bird, everything lying in the grass, any animals like squirrels or chipmunks, dogs or cats, and any people as you turn your head from one side back to the other.

Now it is time. Place your hands over your ears and turn your head very, very slowly from one side to the other. Look very carefully at all there is to see. Then turn your head back to the other side just as slowly. Try to be aware of all there is to see.

(See to it that your children have their hands over their ears as they turn their heads from side to side very slowly. Wait for them to finish, and then ask them to tell you everything they saw. Probe gently for details about color, about shapes, and about even their smallest and most routine observations. When several children are participating, it is both interesting and instructive to listen to all of the observations and to point out how many different things and how many common things were observed by all. Now continue with this script or with your revision of it.)

Return to your breathing now. Relax, breathe out slowly and smoothly. Breathe in and feel your breath enter your nose and reach your expanding belly. Be comfortable. Quietly, close your eyes. For the next minute, listen to all of the sounds around you. Listen for the sounds of birds, insects, wind blowing through the trees, people talking in the distance, people playing, dogs barking, or cats purring. Listen carefully even to the sound of your own breathing. Listen in the stillness and quiet of the next single minute.

(As I have noted previously, there may be some children who do not want to close their eyes. Either go on to the next part of the script, or ask them to remain quiet with their eyes open, while the others do this part of the exercise. Actually time one minute by your watch. It is amazing how long a minute can be when we are mindful of it. At the end of the minute, ask your children to open their eyes, and give them a few seconds to blink and focus. Then continue with my script or your revision of it.)

What did you hear? (Listen to all of their observations. Probe gently to get as many details as possible. Again point out which sounds were heard by many or even all of the participants and which some heard and others did not. After all of the children who wish to share their observations have had the chance, continue with this script or your revised version.)

Do you know how long your eyes were closed? Did it seem to be a short amount of time or a long amount of time? Is there anything anyone wants to say before we continue with the next part of this exercise? (Pause for just a moment to regain a sense of stillness and focus.)

104

Return to your breathing again. Relax. Feel your breath enter your nose and reach down to your belly. Feel your belly expand as you breathe in slowly and smoothly. Then feel it deflate when you breathe out slowly and smoothly. Breathe normally. Just be comfortable. Enjoy these moments outside. Relax. . . .

If you are comfortable with your eyes closed, then please close them for this next part. If you are not, then you can do the rest of the exercise with your eyes open. It is your choice. Do what *you* want to do. The next part will only take another minute. . . .

Enjoy the stillness and calmness of this moment. In this next minute, I will ask you to think about some questions. Please do not answer right now. Just remain silent and still. There will be plenty of time to talk about these questions in just a minute. . . .

Now, in the stillness of this moment, feel the wind. What does it feel like? Is it ticklish? Is it soft? Is it harsh? Is it warm or hot or cool or cold?

Do you feel the sun at all? If you do how does it feel? On what part of your body do you feel it?

What does the ground around you feel like? If you have to reach to touch the soil or the grass, then go ahead, but please remain silent. If your eyes are closed, then keep them closed even now as you feel the ground around you. If your eyes are open, let your fingers feel the ground as you remain quiet and still. If you can, pick up a blade of grass or a rock or some soil. What does it feel like in your hand? Is it smooth or rough? Is it warm or cool? Is it long or short or crumbly?

(After a minute has passed, ask those who have closed their eyes to open them and blink a couple of times. When all of the children are ready, resume your discussion of observations as before. Then continue the script.)

Return to your breathing, and sit comfortably. If you wish, close your eyes for just a minute. It is also okay for you to keep your eyes open for the next minute. Sense how still and how calm you are. Enjoy this moment.

What does the world around you smell like? Do you smell any flowers or plants? Do you smell any grass? Do you smell the breeze? What does it smell like? Do you smell any perfumes? Do you smell any animals?

Spend the next few seconds in silence, and smell all of the scents, all of the aromas, and all of the fragrances you can smell. (Wait about thirty seconds. Ask those who have closed their eyes to open them slowly and blink a few times. Then resume your conversation with your children as before, and continue the script.)

Now we have come to the end of this exercise. As a gift, you will have the next minute to see, hear, touch, and smell the world around you before we conclude. If you wish, keep your eyes or ears closed for this whole minute and simply see the world around you or listen to it. If you wish, do several things. Close your eyes for a moment and listen to the world around you. Put your hands over your ears and look at the world. Touch the ground around you. Feel the sun and the breeze. Smell all that there is to smell. You do what you want to for the next minute. Enjoy your world. Now your minute begins.

(Wait for the full minute. When all of the children are ready, finish your conversation. Ask them for any final observations. Perhaps read from one of the sources I have recommended, or simply take one last long, slow, smooth, deep breath. Remain seated for just a moment to allow for transition, and then get up and return to your home, classroom, or car.)

Service

Over the tomb of Mohandas Karamchand Gandhi, also called Mahatma (The Great Soul), it says: "Think of the poorest person you have ever seen and ask if your next act will be of any use to him." Today, so many people are in need. They are in need of health care, of employment, of housing, of food, of schooling, of companionship, or simply of a kind word. The world around us, the planet that pulses with life and the breath of life, is in need as well. It is in need of biospheric care, of aqua care, and of natural resource care.

For every spiritual tradition, the spiritual life has always included the notion of service expressed variously in deeds that demonstrate love and benevolence to others and to our living planet. In their book *How Can I Help?*, Ram Dass and Paul Gorman remind us that historically the world's great spiritual traditions taught that service was a fundamental facet of our lives while we walk the earth:

> Awakening from our sense of separateness is what we are called to do in all things, not merely service. Whether these traditions speak of us as being cut off from God, Nature, Original Mind, True Being, the Tao, the Dharma—they call on us, in one voice, to undertake the journey back to unity. Service, from this perspective, is part of that journey. It is no longer an end in itself. It is a vehicle through which we reach a deeper understanding of life.[9]

Service helps to restore us to wholeness, and wholeness is one of the etymological bases of the word *holiness*—not just as a nexus of living beings that share a common cosmic abode but as individuals, too. More than eighteen hundred years ago, a rabbi named Akiva taught that "there are 248 positive *mitzvot* ("Thou shall" kinds of commandments in Jewish legal tradition) in the Torah, corresponding to the number of parts in the human body. Each and every part of the body shouts to the person, 'Do a *mitzvah* (in this case meaning a good deed) through me.' "

Akiva associated the performance of service, or *mitzvot*, with our growth toward unity and wholeness: Holiness. It seems to me that what the great spiritual traditions are each saying in many languages and metaphors is that with every breath we take, with every opening of our eyes, with every sound we hear, with every raising of our voices, with every step we take, and with every reaching out of a hand, we have an exalted invitation to participate in the sacred task of moving ourselves and our world closer to wholeness.

What follows are some recommendations for making service a fundamental part of your children's daily lives.

PREPARATION

There are some books that might provide you with ideas that work; they involve varying amounts of time and can easily involve children of all ages in the sacred act of service. The first is a book entitled *Mitzvahs* by Danny Siegel (Pittsboro, NC: The Town House Press, 1990). Even though it carries a Hebrew title, the range of activities and motivating stories found within are appropriate for all ages, genders, and spiritual paths. I also recommend *Kids Who Make A Difference* by Joyce M. Roché, Marie Rodriguez, and Phyllis Schneider (New York: Avon Products, Inc., 1993). It is an action-oriented guide filled with inspiring stories that show what our children can do to make a difference in our world. Additionally, take a look at *Going Green: A Kid's Handbook to Saving the Planet* by John Elkington, Julia Hailes, Douglas Hill, and Joel Makower (New York: Puffin Books, 1990). As you might imagine there is a plethora of environmentally oriented activities for children contained in this book. Another example is *Raising an Earth Friendly Child: The Keys to Your Child's Happy, Healthy Future* by Debbie J. Tilsworth (Fairbanks, AK: Raven Press, 1991). This book, too, contains environmental and "earth-friendly" activities to do with your children.

Aside from these books, the best kind of preparation you can provide your children regarding service to others and to our planet is to make it a part of your lives, too. Children can easily get involved in aspects of your own social action projects. Most local and regional newspapers list organizations that work to serve others. Also, houses of worship in your neighborhood are great sources of projects.

INSTRUCTIONS

Using the resources listed above, find a path of service for your children and for yourself. In this case, class or family cooperation helps to inspire and unify all participants. In my own family, my very young daughter Mikki helps me recycle, make sandwiches for the hungry, and she does one more thing: I have a big collection of pennies, and every morning she gets a chance to reach in and grab what she can. Then she counts them and puts half of whatever she has grabbed into her little "pony bank" and the other half into another bank for the welfare of others. Once every couple of weeks, we take some pennies from both banks (never enough to actually cover the costs involved, but, as you know, that is not the point), and we go to a local bookstore and purchase one book for her and one for the boys and girls of a local prison's center for children.

Indeed, there are so many ways by which service can become a part of our lives. While we know that it is holy in its own right, acts of service can be sanctified by finding prayers from your own spiritual traditions or readings from the great spiritual masters. It is also wonderful to simply pause silently before performing an act of service to ask your children to consider that for the next few moments, their lives will be focused upon helping others or healing their planet. Again, we return to the notion of mindfulness, and a simple silent moment or two focused as suggested may help your children become mindful of the sacred act of service.

Dream Journal

On the average, we spend about one-fifth of our sleeping time dreaming. That would suggest that over the course of a seventy- or eighty-year life, we may spend as many as five or six years dreaming. Perhaps, for some of us that might be even more. It would be unthinkable for us to spend five or six years in classrooms or in the presence of spiritual masters only to ignore whatever insights we might have gained. Yet most of us ignore our dreams or consider them frivolous.

Dreams have not always been so disparaged or discounted. In fact, until quite recently, dreams have fascinated people in all cultures and all historical eras. Once people believed that dreams were important messages containing valuable wisdom for waking life. For instance, the Greeks erected hundreds of temples dedicated to dream incubation. Seekers of dream wisdom journeyed to such temples where typically they would participate in sacred rituals to elicit healing and insightful dreams. And in our own country, Native American shamans once did, and in some places still do, trek deep into the countryside where they induce dreams to bring powerful healing knowledge to their lives and to their people.

In the *Zohar*, often called the "Bible of Kabbalah," we read that a dream not remembered might as well have not been dreamt, and therefore, a dream forgotten and gone from the mind is never fulfilled. In other words, discounting or ignoring our dreams is a missed opportunity to gain valuable insight. Dr. Edward Hoffman considers the practice of recalling and discussing dreams to be a significant aspect of a child's spiritual life.

Unfortunately, as Hoffman observes, our contemporary culture discourages the practice of dream work:

> From our earliest years, we are taught either to ignore our dreams completely or to dismiss them as inherently trivial. Almost never are children encouraged to remember and relate their dreams. By adhering to this attitude as we reach adulthood, we inevitably fragment ourselves and lose touch with a valuable source of inspiration.[10]

In his book, *Visions of Innocence*, Hoffman encourages us adults to share our dreams with our children so they will be encouraged to share them with us. A Dream Journal is one way to share dream work.

One of the pioneers in the creation of journal exercises for children is Lucia Capacchione. Her book *The Creative Journal for Children: A Guide for Parents, Teachers, and Counselors* is a classic of its kind, and I recommend its use to expand your repertoire of dream work exercises for children. For centuries upon centuries, some of the greatest spiritual masters have kept dream journals. With the help of Capacchione and Hoffman, perhaps our children will develop this spiritual habit.

PREPARATION

Shop with your children for a large notebook with blank pages. See which ones most attract your children, and once you return home, invite them to make it truly theirs by decorating it, illustrating its cover, or wrapping it with paper they have selected. Ownership and confidentiality are important issues with this kind of work. So, in addition to designing it, invite your children to write their names upon its cover or just inside. Help the younger children with this. I found that even before my daughter Mikki began writing, she loved to trace. Consequently, in those early days when she was requested to place her name on a card or project, I wrote it for her lightly in pencil. Then she selected any marker, crayon, or colored pencil she desired and traced what I had written. I recall how proud she felt as she boasted of writing her own name. Maybe this will be the case for your little ones, too.

Let your children or students know that whatever is written in this journal belongs to them only; you will always be happy to see or read anything they include in their journals, but only when they want this. Since, however, you want to discuss their dreams with them *while sharing your own* (that is only fair, after all), you might ask their permission to see what they had to say or draw about their dreams. In all sense of fairness, it would seem more equitable if you kept a dream journal, too. In fact, your willingness to share from your own journal might embolden them and enthuse them to share theirs with you. Dreams may be a vehicle for spiritual wisdom and insight, but the heartfelt sharing and demonstrating of your own respect for dreams (or any of the spiritual exercises contained in this book, for that matter) is spirituality in action. Acts of spiritual integrity prove to be among the deepest and most abiding imprints upon the souls of our children.

INSTRUCTIONS

Here are some recommendations on how you might help your children keep a Dream Journal. It is not necessary to make an entry in a Dream Journal every day. Let your psyche (as in soul) impel you to write and/or draw about a dream. In advance, you might guide your children to keep their journals and writing/drawing implements by their beds so they can make their entries as soon upon arising as possible. If they are not comfortable with this, try to guide them to make their entries before breakfast: as the hours pass, dreams become more and more ephemeral. They fade from our consciousness like early morning mist evaporates as the sun climbs in the sky. It is possible, however, that a discussion over the breakfast table about dreams might induce them to make their entries, too. For some children, it is right to make their entries upon arising. For others, the time might be anytime before breakfast. For still others, it might be after a good breakfast of warm food and delicious dream dialogue.

If your children wish you to help them make their entries, try to do so in a way that grants them some sign of respect for their confidentiality and appreciation for the honor and trust they have afforded you. Now, what kind of entries am I talking about? All kinds. Drawings of significant images that arose in their dreams, for instance. Encourage your children to use whatever colors they choose or no colors at all. Thoughts about issues that they recall are other kinds of entries. Maybe they have questions about something; questions are yet another kind of entry. Maybe they recall feelings that came up for them in their dreams. Encourage them to write about what they felt and/or to draw those feelings. Give the feelings representation in images with or without colors.

I believe that it is valuable for children to date their entries and sign each one as a way of owning them. It is perfectly fine if some entries take pages while others take inches. In my opinion, it is valuable to try and include both images and words about the drawings to whatever extent is possible and comfortable. Even little children can talk with you about what they have drawn. With their permission, you can write some key words or thoughts for them and even help them write the date and their names.

If dreams become part of some of your usual conversations with your children, then their wisdom will naturally become known. In Hoffman's book, some of the most powerful spiritual experiences he came across in his research were dreams experienced by his adult respondents during their childhoods. The Dream Journal is one vehicle for encouraging our children to become comfortable with this spiritual dimension. Perhaps they will even grow to discover some of the remarkable wisdom that graces us through the imagery of our dreams.

The Evocative Word Exercise

Roberto Assagioli (1888–1974) was an Italian medical doctor and psychiatrist who evolved a school of psychotherapy that he called

Psychosynthesis. Assagioli was a contemporary of Freud and Jung; in fact, he was instrumental in introducing psychoanalysis to Italy. I consider Psychosynthesis to be rather unique among types of psychotherapies: it is open to the wisdom of other schools, it lacks dogmatism, and it has a spiritual dimension that places it among the psychotherapies that have come to be called transpersonal.

It was Assagioli's conviction that we "live in a septic psychic climate or atmosphere by which we are constantly being contaminated."[11] Assagioli taught that we might neutralize the toxic effects of this septic climate on ourselves and our children by exposure "to beneficent and constructive stimuli and influences."[12] One such antiseptic option available to us and to our children is the use of words.

"That words have their effects on our mood and ideas does not require demonstration. Words are symbols that not only indicate or point out objects or psychic facts, but that also possess the power of stimulating and arousing activity associated with them. They 'evoke' and make operative the meanings and *idées-forces* that they signify."[13] Indeed, Assagioli reminded his readers that they lived, as we do today, among industries like the advertising industry that know just how powerful words are and how effectively they arouse activities and ideas associated with them. How true! Are there any parents who have not witnessed the power of advertising on their children?

While his technique of evocative words was created within the framework of a psychotherapeutic philosophy, this exercise was not conceived for clinical psychological use alone. As a matter of fact, Assagioli also envisioned educational uses for this method—in the classroom and even in the home.[14]

The exercise I have included here is my adaptation of Assagioli's technique for family and classroom applications. Given the polluting and spiritually toxic nature of many of the environments in which we and our children live daily, the home or classroom can provide just the remedies we need.

PREPARATION

To begin, create cards, large or small, on which a key word is written. Make sure that only one word is written per card. Assagioli himself recommended seventeen words printed in particular colors: Calm (dark green);

Comprehension (yellow); Confidence (reddish orange); Courage (red); Energy (brick red); Enthusiasm (brick red); Goodness (gold); Gratitude (gold); Harmony (green); Joy (yellow); Love (blue); Patience (green); Serenity (deep blue); Silence (blue); Simplicity (gold); Will (red); Wisdom (dark blue). It was his recommendation, as well, that the words be printed in capital letters.[15] You be the judge of what works best in your home or classroom.

You may, of course, substitute key words of your own or add others with significant evocative potential for you and your children. For instance, you might want to add a word like *healing* or *health* and print it in a color you consider particularly appropriate.

For children too young to read these words or comprehend them, you might draw or find a picture that represents their meanings visually. In fact, it is possible that for those adults or older children who are very visually oriented, the picture cards might prove to be powerfully evocative.

INSTRUCTIONS

Once you have created your cards, place them around the home where they will be seen regularly. It is especially impressive for a card and color that have great value for you to be among the first visual stimuli you perceive in beginning and ending your day. For example, you might put one on your bathroom mirror, on the cabinet above your sink, on the ceiling above your bed, on the wall you turn to face upon arising in the morning, on the refrigerator, above the television, in your car, in your office, in your locker, and so on. It is your choice whether or not to make several copies of the same evocative word or picture, to rotate cards around the house, or even to change them completely from time to time.

Every now and then, I advise that you and your children share your reflections about these cards and what they mean to you. You might also want to try experimenting with these cards as the primary external visual foci of your meditations or as the bases of imaginal journeys.

Planting the Seeds of Esteem

In the preceding exercise, the eminent psychiatrist Roberto Assagioli made clear that we are surrounded daily by septic psycho-spiritual contagions that often assume forms such as disapproval, harsh criticism, judgment by self and others, lack of love, and punishment. His technique used evocative words as antiseptics of sorts.

I, too, believe that words can heal, and they can harm. In addition to our own spoken and contemplative affirmations of ourselves, it is powerful for significant others in our lives to value us and say so in words and deeds. The book's final exercise enables children to affirm themselves in a potent and organic way, and it also grants the significant others in our children's lives—us—the power to esteem them and plant within them seeds of worth and well-being.

More than twenty years ago, my good friend and best-selling author Barbara Hoberman Levine was a young woman with a career and a young family. Then she discovered that she had a massive, life-threatening brain tumor and began her journey toward the healing that comes with wholeness of mind and body, spirit and flesh. In fact, Barbara, who is a constant source of inspiration and education in my life, learned that septic language can bring "dis-ease" of the body, the mind, and the soul. In her extraordinary book *Your Body Believes Every Word You Say*, she writes:

> Words are often the trigger (catalyst) that lead to the symptoms of disease: you are what you think, feel, and say about yourself. You are what you believe about you. . . . A *seedthought* is a significant catalyst for a physical or emotional response. A seedthought is a thought you think frequently that either emanates from, or creates, your core beliefs. Just as the apple core contains the seeds that sprout into an apple tree, you have at your core, beliefs that shape you.[16]

Almost seven centuries earlier, the Christian mystic Johannes Eckhart, also known as Meister Eckhart, presaged Levine's observations with these words:

> The seed of God is in us. Given an intelligent and hard-working farmer and a diligent field hand, it will thrive and grow up to God, whose seed it is; and accordingly its fruits will be God-nature. Pear seeds grow into pear trees, nut seeds into nut trees, and God seed into God.

Most assuredly, we hold many of the seeds, either of esteem or contempt, that we sow into the growing hearts of our children.

Certain seedthoughts can harm our children's growth and spiritual health, and others can enrich and support them. This exercise is an opportunity for you to plant seeds of esteem and spiritual potency in the hearts and souls of your children, and it gives them a chance to learn to do the same for themselves.

This exercise uses seeds and flowers for several additional spiritual reasons. It is well-known that seeds historically have represented the potentiality from whose core the Cosmic Tree grows. Also, in Hindu tradition, the seed is understood as the Divine Spirit, *Atman,* at the center of our being. It is the heart.[17]

As seeds grow into the flowers they are destined to become, they are either nourished by their environment or injured by it. We create the psycho-spiritual environments in which our children grow. The flowers used in this exercise are five-petaled flowers. Ancient masters considered flowers, in general, to represent potentiality in the bud and manifest development in their opening. More specifically, these same masters taught that five-petaled flowers symbolized both the "Gardens of the Blessed" and the microcosm of the human being "fixed in the five extremities of the five senses."[18]

All of the flowers recommended in this exercise are five-petaled flowers that come in packets of seeds and are readily available everywhere. It is my hope that this exercise will be a vehicle for planting positive, affirming seedthoughts in your children, and that it will give them living symbols of beauty and vitality that will serve visually to reinforce their sense of self-esteem and spiritual health.

PREPARATION

Obtain large flower pots for you and all of the children who are participating, potting soil, and packets of any of the following seeds: Blue Flax, Baby White Impatiens, Four O' Clocks, Nicotiana.[19] All of these seeds can be obtained from local nurseries or hardware stores. Purchase one packet for you and one packet for each of the children. While the packets can be the same, it might be nice to have different kinds of flowers growing. You might wish to allow your children to select which flower they want to plant. All of the packets have pictures of the mature flowers on their fronts. If you would like to choose other flowers that are grown from seeds and that are five-petaled, consult your local florist or nursery. To tend the flowers as they sprout forth from the seeds, follow the directions on the packets.

In the beginning, you will have a flower pot for yourself, and each child will have his/her own as well. Fill the pots with the necessary amount of soil. Gather together with your child(ren), your seeds, and your flower pots filled with soil.

The following script is my recommendation, although, as always, feel free to revise it to best meet the various needs of your children. Since I offer you examples of seedthoughts of esteem at the end of the script, I advise you to read it all through once or twice in order to determine how best to use it. The script for this exercise reads as follows:

You are a very special child (or very special children). Because you bring beauty and happiness to my life, I thought we would plant a special kind of flower that, when it grows, will bring beauty and happiness to the world, just as you do. Open your bag(s) of seeds and spill all of the seeds in front of you and your pot(s). (Pause for this to be done.)

Now take a few seeds in your hand(s). I want to tell you something I think is very special about you. After I do, I will ask you to repeat my words with me and press the seeds in your hand(s) into the soil. For instance, I think you are special because you...

Now as you press some of your seeds into the soil in your pot(s), please repeat what I have said. Join with me: I am special because I...

That is great. Make sure to press your seeds under the soil until they are completely covered. Good. Now, I also think you are special because...

Take some more seeds in your hand(s) and join with me: I am special because...

And now press those seeds into the soil along with the others. Terrific. Take some more seeds in your hands, and get ready to plant them, after I tell you that you are also special because...

Press those seeds into the soil as you join with me and say, I am special because...

Now take the rest of the seeds in your hand(s). I want you to know that I love (like) you so much because...

Now press the rest of the seeds into the soil as you say, I am so lovable (likable) because...

Here are some seedthoughts of esteem and affirmation which you may want to use to fill the ellipses above. As always, feel free to adapt these or allow your heart to speak your own words. My litany of affirmations consists of the following: you make me smile/you help me around the house/you are a good brother or sister/you study hard in school/you share nicely with others/you give good hugs and kisses/you help keep the earth clean/you are a good ballplayer/you are a good dancer/you are a good pianist/you are a good artist/you are a good friend to your friends/you are a good cook/you are a good swimmer/you make up great stories/you have a terrific imagination/you are wonderfully sensitive and caring/you take good care of your dog/you take good care of your cat/you do many great things to help the environment/you are a good reader/you are a great son/you are a great daughter/you are great students/you are a great grandson/you are a great granddaughter/you are great grandchildren.

Help your children care for their plants in the days and months to come. As the seeds begin to sprout, remind them of all of the ways they bring joy to your life, of all of the things they do for you, for the planet, and for others that are so appreciated, and of all of the reasons you love them as much as you do.

Follow-Up Activities

In general, follow-up activities for any of the exercises contained in this book might involve drawing pictures of any of the images that arose during meditations or imaginal journeys. If your children or students can write, invite them to write down some key thoughts about what they drew and/or experienced. If they are unable to write, invite them to tell you about what they felt or experienced, and write down their thoughts for them. Discuss them, display them, or just let them be. If you choose to strike up a conversation with your children about what they felt or perceived during the exercises, personal experience has taught me that your children will be more inclined to share with you if you share with them what the exercises were like for you.

Perhaps you may choose to tell a story after an exercise. You might also opt to play music and to invite your children to recline and relax to the rhythms and sounds. Don Campbell's recommendations about relaxing music are especially pertinent here. Maybe the most basic way to bring an exercise session to a conclusion is simply to remain seated in silence and allow the wonderfully delicious tranquility and stillness to surround you for as long as you like. Experiment with these follow-up activities and create your own. Most important, enjoy!

NOTES

1. Daniel Goleman, *The Meditative Mind* (Los Angeles: Jeremy P. Tarcher, 1982), p. 106.

2. Rev. Jiyu Kennett, Roshi, "The Education of the Buddhist Child," in *Spiritual Parenting in the New Age,* ed. Anne Carson (Freedom, CA: The Crossing Press, 1989), p. 23.

3. Kennett, p. 23.

4. Maureen Murdock, *Spinning Inward: Using Guided Imagery with Children for Learning, Creativity, & Relaxation* (Boston: Shambhala Publications, 1987), p. 16.

5. Deborah Rozman, *Meditation for Children,* 2nd ed. (Boulder Creek, CA: Planetary Publications, 1989), pp. 65–66.

6. Anthony de Mello, *Sadhana: A Way to God* (Garden City, NY: Image Books, 1984), p. 17.

7. Matthew Fox, *Creation Spirituality: Liberating Gifts for the Peoples of the Earth* (San Francisco: HarperSanFrancisco, 1991), p. 11.

8. Fox, p. 11.

9. Ram Dass and Paul Gorman, *How Can I Help? Stories and Reflections on Service* (New York: Alfred A. Knopf, 1991), p. 224.

10. Edward Hoffman, *Visions of Innocence: Spiritual and Inspirational Experiences of Childhood* (Boston: Shambhala Publications, 1992), p. 162.

11. Roberto Assagioli, "The Technique of Evocative Words," *Human Dimensions 3* (Winter 1974): 8.

12. Assagioli, p. 8.

13. Assagioli, p. 8.

14. Assagioli, p. 8.

15. Assagioli, p. 9.

16. Barbara Hoberman Levine, *Your Body Believes Every Word You Say* (Boulder Creek, CA: Aslan Publishing, 1991), pp. 49–50.

17. J. C. Cooper, *An Illustrated Encyclopedia of Traditional Symbols* (London: Thames and Hudson, 1978), p. 146.

18. J. C. Cooper, p. 70.

19. I wish to thank Miss Tigger Mann of Pinchbeck Brothers Florist and Nursery, in Ridgefield, Connecticut, for helping me identify some of the five-petaled flowers for this exercise.

Bibliography and Resources

List of Works Cited

Assagioli, Roberto. "The Technique of Evocative Words." *Human Dimensions* 3, no. 4 (Winter 1974): 8–9.

Autumn, Diane. "Ecology and Spirituality." *Seeds of Unfolding* 9, no. 1 (1992): 4–7.

Ballentine, Rudolph, M., ed. *The Theory and Practice of Meditation*. 2nd ed. Honesdale, PA: The Himalayan International Institute of Yoga Science and Philosophy of the USA, 1986.

Belansky, Della. "Parenthood as Spiritual Training." *A Theosophical Guide for Parents*, pp. 25–26. 336 South Pueblo Ave., Ojai, CA 93203: Parents Theosophical Research Group, 1981.

Berends, Polly Berrien. *Whole Child/Whole Parent*. rev. ed. New York: Harper & Row Publishers, 1987.

Blank, William. *Torah, Tarot & Tantra: A Guide to Jewish Spiritual Growth*. Boston: Coventure, 1991.

Campbell, Don. *Music: Physician for Times to Come*. Wheaton, IL: Quest Books, 1991.

———. *Music and Miracles*. Wheaton, IL: Quest Books, 1992.

Capacchione, Lucia. *The Creative Journal for Children: A Guide for Parents, Teachers, and Counselors.* Boston: Shambhala Publications, 1982.

Carroll, David. *Spiritual Parenting.* New York: Paragon House, 1990.

Carson, Anne, ed. *Spiritual Parenting in the New Age.* Freedom, CA: The Crossing Press, 1989.

Cooper, J. C. *An Illustrated Encyclopedia of Traditional Symbols.* London: Thames and Hudson, 1978.

Cornell, Joseph. *Sharing Nature with Children: A Parents' and Teachers' Nature-Awareness Guidebook.* Nevada City, CA: Ananda Publications, 1979.

————. *Sharing the Joy of Nature.* Nevada City, CA: Dawn Publications, 1989.

Dass, Baba Hari. *A Child's Garden of Yoga.* P.O. Box 2550, Santa Cruz, CA 95063: A Sri Rama Publishing/Hanuman Fellowship Book, 1980.

Dass, Ram, and Paul Gorman. *How Can I Help? Stories and Reflections on Service.* New York: Alfred A. Knopf, 1991.

de Mello, Anthony. *Sadhana: A Way to God.* Garden City, NY: Image Books, 1984.

————. *The Heart of the Enlightened: A Book of Story Meditations.* New York: Doubleday Books, 1989.

de Mille, Richard. *Put Your Mother on the Ceiling.* New York: Penguin Books, 1976.

Elkind, David. *The Hurried Child: Growing Up Too Fast Too Soon.* Reading, MA: Addison-Wesley Publishing Company, 1981.

————. "Spirituality in Education." *Holistic Education Review* 5, no. 1 (Spring 1992): 12–16.

Epstein, Gerald. *Healing Visualizations.* New York: Bantam Books, 1989.

Ferrucci, Piero. *What We May Be.* Los Angeles: Jeremy P. Tarcher, 1982.

Gardner, Howard. *Frames of Mind: The Theory of Multiple Intelligences.* New York: Basic Books, 1983.

Goldberg, Hillel. "Just Talking." *Intermountain Jewish News* (October 30, 1992): 2.

Goleman, Daniel. *The Meditative Mind: The Varieties of Meditative Experience.* Los Angeles: Jeremy P. Tarcher, 1982.

Green, Arthur, ed. *Jewish Spirituality: From the Bible through the Middle Ages.* New York: The Crossroad Publishing Co., 1986.

Hanh, Thich Nhat. *The Miracle of Mindfulness: A Manual on Meditation.* Boston: Beacon Press, 1987.

Hendricks, Gay, and Thomas B. Roberts. *The Second Centering Book.* New York: Prentice Hall Press, 1977.

Heschel, Abraham Joshua. *God in Search of Man: A Philosophy of Judaism.* New York: Farrar, Straus, and Giroux, 1958.

Hoffman, Edward. *Visions of Innocence: Spiritual and Inspirational Experiences of Childhood.* Boston: Shambhala Publications, 1992.

Kaplan, Aryeh. *Jewish Meditation: A Practical Guide.* New York: Schocken Books, 1985.

Khan, Hazrat Inayat. *Education from Before Birth to Maturity.* Geneva, Switzerland: Sufi Publishing Co., 1962.

Kornfield, Jack. "A Parent's Guide to Conscious Childraising: Conscious Parenting." *Common Boundary* 2, no. 1 (January/February 1993): 23–29.

Krishnamurti, Jiddu. *Education and the Significance of Life.* San Francisco: Harper & Row, 1981.

Kurtz, Ernest, and Katherine Ketcham. *The Spirituality of Imperfection: Modern Wisdom from Classic Sources.* New York: Bantam Books, 1992.

Kushner, Lawrence. *The Book of Miracles.* New York: UAHC Press, 1987.

Lindbergh, Anne Morrow. *Gift from the Sea.* New York: Vintage Books, 1991.

Milicevic, Barbara. *Your Spiritual Child.* Marina del Rey, CA: DeVorss & Company, 1984.

Miller, John P. "Toward a Spiritual Curriculum." *Holistic Education Review* 5, no. 1 (Spring 1992): 43–50.

Montagu, Ashley. *Growing Young.* New York: McGraw-Hill Book Company, 1981.

Montessori, Maria. *Education for a New World.* Madras, India: Kalakshetra, 1963.

———. *The Absorbent Mind.* Madras, India: Kalakshetra, 1973.

Murdock, Maureen. *Spinning Inward: Using Guided Imagery with Children for Learning, Creativity, & Relaxation.* Boston: Shambhala Publications, 1987.

Rosman, Steven M. "The Power of Story." *Hadassah Magazine* 73, no. 5 (January 1992): 32–34.

123

Rozman, Deborah. *Meditation for Children.* 2nd ed. Boulder Creek, CA: Planetary Publications, 1989.

Smith, Huston. *The Religions of Man.* New York: HarperPerennial, 1986.

Van Matre, Steve, and Bill Weiler, eds. *The Earth Speaks.* Box 288, Warrenville, IL: The Institute for Earth Education, 1983.

Welwood, John. "The Healing Power of Unconditional Presence." *The Quest* 5, no. 4 (Winter 1992): 35–40.

Books for Additional Reading

Armstrong, Thomas. *The Radiant Child.* Wheaton, IL: Theosophical Publishing House, 1985.

Bailey, Covert, and Lea Bishop. *Target Recipes.* Boston: Houghton Mifflin Company, 1985.

Bennett, J. G. *Gurdjieff: A Very Great Enigma.* York Beach, ME: Samuel Weiser, 1973.

Benson, Herbert. *The Relaxation Response.* New York: Avon Books, 1975.

———, Eileen M. Stuart, and Associates at the Mind/Body Medical Institute of the New England Deaconess Hospital and Harvard Medical School. *The Wellness Book: The Comprehensive Guide to Maintaining Health and Treating Stress-Related Illness.* New York: Birch Lane Press (Carol Publishing Group), 1992.

Berends, Polly Berrien. *Gently Lead: How to Teach Your Children About God While Finding Out for Yourself.* New York: HarperPerennial, 1992.

Brother Lawrence. *The Practice of the Presence of God.* White Plains, NY: Peter Pauper Press, 1963.

Buxbaum, Yitzhak. *Jewish Spiritual Practices.* Northvale, NJ: Jason Aronson, 1990.

Buzan, Tony. *Use Both Sides of Your Brain.* New York: E. P. Dutton & Co., 1976.

Carse, James P. *Finite and Infinite Games: A Vision of Life as Play and Possibility.* New York: The Free Press, 1986.

Carson, Rachel. *The Sense of Wonder.* New York: Harper & Row, 1965.

Clarke, Jean Illsley. *Self-Esteem: A Family Affair.* San Francisco: HarperSanFrancisco, 1978.

Cohen, Kenneth K. *Imagine That! A Child's Guide to Yoga.* Illus. Joan Hyme. Santa Barbara: Santa Barbara Books, 1983.

Cohen, Michael J. *How Nature Works.* Box 640, Meetinghouse Road, Walpole, NH: Stillpoint Publishing, 1988.

Ecumenical Task Force on Christian Education for World Peace. *Try This: Family Adventures Toward Shalom.* Nashville: Discipleship Resources, 1979.

Feldman, Christina, and Jack Kornfield, eds. *Stories of the Spirit, Stories of the Heart.* San Francisco: HarperSanFrancisco, 1991.

Fitzpatrick, Jean Grasso. *Something More: Nurturing Your Child's Spiritual Growth.* New York: Viking, 1991.

Garth, Maureen. *Starbright: Meditations for Children.* San Francisco: HarperSanFrancisco, 1991.

Greenbaum, Avraham. *Under the Table & How to Get Up: Jewish Pathways of Spiritual Growth.* New York: Tsohar Publishing, 1991.

Hanh, Thich Nhat. *Peace is Every Step: The Path of Mindfulness in Everyday Life.* New York: Bantam Books, 1991.

Harp, David. *The Three Minute Meditator.* San Francisco: mind's i press, 1987.

Heller, David. *Talking to Your Child About God: A Book for Families of All Faiths.* New York: Bantam Books, 1990.

Hidden Villa Environmental Education. *Manure to Meadow to Milkshake.* Hidden Villa, Inc., Drawer AH, Los Altos, CA, 1978.

Hoffman, Edward. *The Heavenly Ladder, Kabbalistic Techniques for Inner Growth.* P.O. Box 540, East Meadow, NY 11554: Four Worlds Press, 1985.

Houston, Jean. *The Possible Human: A Course in Extending Your Physical, Mental, and Creative Abilities.* Los Angeles: Jeremy P. Tarcher, 1982.

Jenkins, Peggy D. *Joyful Child: New Age Activities to Enhance Children's Joy.* New York: Dodd, Mead, 1988.

Johnson, Carolyn M. *Discovering Nature with Young People: An Annotated Bibliography and Selection Guide.* Westport, CT: Greenwood Press, 1987.

Kennedy, Eugene. *Tomorrow's Catholics/Yesterday's Church: The Two Cultures of American Catholicism.* New York: Harper & Row Publishers, 1988.

Kennett, Jiyu (Roshi), Swami Radha, and Robert Frager. "How to Be a Transpersonal Teacher Without Becoming a Guru." *Journal of Transpersonal Psychology* 7, no. 1 (1975): 48–65.

Knapp, Clifford E., and Joel Goodman. *Humanizing Environmental Education*. Martinsville, IN: American Camping Association, 1981.

Kushi, Michio. *The Macrobiotic Way: The Complete Macrobiotic Diet and Exercise Book*. Wayne, NJ: Avery Publishing Group, 1985.

Kushner, Lawrence. *God was in this Place and i, I Did Not Know*. Woodstock, VT: Jewish Lights Publishing, 1991.

Langford, Cricket. *Meditation for Little People*. Novato, CA: Inner Light Foundation, 1974.

Levine, Barbara Hoberman. *Your Body Believes Every Word You Say*. Boulder Creek, CA: Aslan Publishing, 1991.

Muir, John. *The Wilderness of John Muir*. Boston: Houghton Mifflin Publishers, 1954.

———. *Stickeen*. Berkeley: Heyday Books, 1981.

Occhiogrosso, Peter. *Through The Labyrinth: Stories of the Search for Spiritual Transformation in Everyday Life*. New York: Viking, 1991.

Pearce, Joseph Chilton. *Magical Child: Rediscovering Nature's Plan for Our Children*. New York: Bantam Books, 1980.

———. *Magical Child Matures*. New York: Dutton, 1985.

Ram Dass, Baba. "One Pointedness of Mind and Teachers as Conveyers of the Universe." *The Only Dance There Is*. New York: Anchor-Doubleday, 1974, pp.93–99.

Rosen, Steven. *Food for the Spirit: Vegetarianism and the World's Religions*. 5286B East Gate Mall, San Diego, CA 92121: Bala/Entourage Books, 1990.

Rosen-Sawyer, Fran, and Bonnie Maltby. *Yoga and Meditation for Children*. RFD#1, Box 121-C, Madison, VA 22727: Fivefold Path, 1983. (Teacher's guide also available.)

Scott, Julian. *Natural Medicine for Children*. New York: Avon Books, 1990.

Sinetar, Marsha. *Ordinary People as Monks and Mystics: Lifestyles for Self-Discovery*. New York: Paulist Press, 1986.

Stein, David E., ed. *A Garden of Choice Fruit: 200 Classic Jewish Quotes on Human Beings and the Environment*. Wyncote, PA: Shomrei Adama (Keepers of the Earth), 1991.

Steiner, Rudolph. *Soul Economy and Waldorf Education*. New York: Anthroposophic Press, 1986.

Trungpa, Chogyam. *Meditation in Action*. Boston: Shambhala Publications, 1969.

Walters, J. Donald. *Education for Life*. Nevada City, CA: Crystal Clarity Publishers, 1986.

Weil, Andrew. *Natural Health, Natural Medicine*. Boston: Houghton Mifflin Company, 1990.

Yoga for Children with Sri Swami Satchidananda. VHS video tape produced by Integral Yoga Communications, Shakicom, Buckingham, VA 23921.

Storytelling Resources

This is far from an exhaustive list, but it will get you started. There may be other books you will add as you explore the shelves of bookstores and libraries. I am sure, however, that from among your own favorites, my suggestions, and the recommendations of librarians, bookstore owners, friends, and others, you will assemble a treasury of precious books.

While many of the books suggested here have been designated for a particular age group, it is my advice that you experiment with books that may be indicated for children older or even younger than your own. Sometimes very simple stories meant for younger children become favorites, and sometimes your children are ready to stretch a bit beyond the recommended reading level. I strongly suggest that you test these tales on your children and let them be the judge of what they like and what they do not, and what they can understand and what they cannot yet. Like actuarial tables, reading lists are compiled according to formulas reflecting a general population, and they may not always provide the best choices for your children.

GENERAL RESOURCES

Bauer, Caroline Heller. *Handbook for Storytellers*. This is a comprehensive and basic book that will provide advice for both the beginning storyteller and the veteran about activities to enhance your storytelling sessions, tips about telling stories, and resources for going further.

Cathon, Laura E., Marion McC. Haushalter, and Virginia A. Russell. *Stories to Tell to Children: A Selected List*. This is a standard reference work that recommends stories for all ages and settings. These tales have been tested in the field for interest, popularity, and quality.

Greene, Ellin, and George Shannon. *Storytelling: A Selected Annotated Bibliography*. In my opinion, this is the best bibliography for storytelling ever assembled. It includes recommendations for storytelling in a variety of professional and nonprofessional settings, a section about the art and techniques of storytelling, and annotated references for storytelling to a variety of listeners: from the very youngest children to children with special needs to the elderly.

Harrison, Annette. *Easy to Tell Stories* (available through NAPPS). This is a collection of twelve lively tales adapted from traditional stories from all over the world and created especially for anyone who wants to tell stories to children. Each story includes notes suggesting ways to enhance your storytelling, recommendations regarding use of voice and gestures, and activities to enrich the experience.

MacGuire, Jack. *Creative Storytelling*. This is another good book for those who want to know more about how to choose stories, how to gear stories toward children of different ages and interests, how to invent them from scratch, how to enhance storytelling skills, and how to enrich stories with activities.

Sawyer, Ruth. *The Way of the Storyteller*. This is a classic book on the way of a western storyteller told by one of the legends of western storytelling. In this unique text, Sawyer reveals the secrets of her art and tells eleven of her best-loved stories. Along the way she describes the pitfalls that await the novice, the triumphs that grace one who perseveres, and the great heights to which storytelling takes the one who tells and the one who hears the tale.

Smith, Charles A. *From Wonder to Wisdom: Using Stories to Help Children Grow*. Professor Smith has categorized and commented upon hundreds of children's books and offers his advice about telling stories, creating your own tales, and introducing stories with difficult and complex themes. This book is one of my own primary resources.

ANTHOLOGIES

These anthologies contain stories that *generally* will be enjoyed most by children in the middle school grades and beyond (approximately ages nine and up). Yet many can be adapted in ways that will bring joy and wonder to the hearts of younger children, too. So if you have younger children, take a look at these books and see for yourself if you can use their tales.

Cole, Joanna. *Best-Loved Folktales of the World*. This is an exception to my prefatory remarks and is truly a book for all ages and all backgrounds. Cole has compiled two hundred tales from all over the world, and she has indexed them according to age, type, theme, and so on.

Feldman, Christina, and Jack Kornfield. *Stories of the Spirit, Stories of the Heart: Parables of the Spiritual Path from Around the World*. This collection gathers stories from the great traditions of the East and the West. There are Chasidic tales, Christian tales, Sufi tales, Native American tales, African tales, Zen tales, Hindu tales, Buddhist tales, among others. These are teaching stories taught by great masters and arranged in subject-oriented sections. Some of the tales are very short, and some are longer. Some are humorous, and some are sober in tone.

Frankel, Ellen. *The Classic Tales: 4,000 Years of Jewish Lore*. Frankel, a master storyteller, has collected over three hundred Jewish tales that span three continents and four millennia. The sources for these tales of wisdom, mystery, laughter, struggle, hope, tradition, and courage have been drawn from all the varied sources of Jewish literature and retold in a marvelous contemporary storytelling style.

Martin, Rafe. *The Hungry Tigress: Buddhist Legends and Jataka Tales*. A collection of classical legends, cautionary tales, and teaching tales that bring to us the wisdom of Buddhism.

Shah, Idries. *Wisdom of the Idiots*. A carefully chosen selection of illustrative anecdotes and tales used in Sufi teaching.

PICTURE BOOKS FOR YOUNG CHILDREN (AGES FOUR TO EIGHT)

Aliki. *The Two of Them*. This is a story about a loving relationship between a grandfather and a granddaughter, and her eventual acceptance of his death and life's continuity.

Anno, Mitsumasa. *Topsy-Turvies: Pictures to Stretch the Imagination.* Some have called Anno's illustrations in this book Escher-like. Certainly, gazing into them and wondering about them will provide a good stretch to any child's imaginal muscle.

Berger, Barbara. *Grandfather Twilight.* This is a poetic and beautifully illustrated story about the routine nocturnal miracle of the arrival of evening. All who listen to this tale and gaze into its illustrations will be comforted by the gentle words and the reassuring message that twilight is a friendly and tender time of the day.

Bogot, Howard, Joyce Orkand, and Robert Orkand. *Gates of Wonder.* This is a special kind of Jewish devotional prayer book for very young children. Lavishly illustrated with a minimum of text, it conveys the wonders of the spiritual realm and is intended as a child's very first Jewish prayer book.

Borack, Barbara. *Grandpa.* This is the story of a little girl who describes her feelings for her grandfather as a result of the experiences they share.

Buscaglia, Leo F. *The Fall of Freddy the Leaf.* This is a beautiful, loving tale about change and death based upon the natural cycle of a leaf during the seasons of the year.

Cooney, Barbara. *Miss Rumphius.* It seems that once upon a time, a long time ago, a young girl was bidden by her grandfather to do something to make the world a more beautiful place. This is the story of that young girl and the surprising discovery she makes years later.

Curtis, Chara, and Cynthia Aldrich. *All I See is Part of Me.* This is a wonderful book that teaches the spiritual lesson of the oneness of all existence. With gorgeous illustrations and beautiful verse, Curtis and Aldrich are able to convey the message that the answers we seek in life are actually much closer than we might think.

———. *Fun is a Feeling.* This inspiring book invites a child to enter a world of fun and fantasy that helps him or her discover that the joys of life begin within.

———. *What You Can See You Can Be!* With delightful verse, this book inspires young children to think positively.

Dharma Publishing. *Jataka Tales Series.* These are individual tales, first told by Buddha, that teach the power of compassion and wisdom. The tales are replete with full-page color illustrations.

Khan, Noor Inayat. *Twenty Jataka Tales.* Here is a terrific selection of Buddhist adventure tales teaching nonviolence and compassion.

Lenzen, Hans Georg. *The Blue Marble.* This is a story about a quiet boy who is given a marble that stimulates his imagination. Then, in turn, he hands it on to another child.

Mayo, Gretchen Will. *Star Tales.* This book contains North American Indian legends about the stars and the constellations.

McNulty, Faith. *The Lady and the Spider.* When a gardener spares the life of a spider, a great lesson is learned about the value of all life.

Pandell, Karen, and Marty Noble. *By Day and By Night.* This story affirms for children that, whether they are awake or asleep, every part of the natural world is in harmony and balance with every other part, and that they are one with their world.

Pappas, Michael G. *Sweet Dreams for Little Ones.* Here are eighteen marvelous and tender fantasy tales that create an atmosphere of warmth and happiness before sleep. In a unique way, your child becomes the central character of stories that build self-esteem and loving relationships.

Pfister, Marcus. *The Rainbow Fish.* An exquisitely illustrated fable about learning to share and the gift of giving.

Pilkey, Dav. *When Cats Dream.* A delightful story filled with fun and fantasy about what might happen when cats dream.

Rosman, Steven. *Deena the Damselfly.* A gentle parable about life, transformation, and metamorphosis. Some have found this book to be a tender aid in helping children process experiences of death.

Sendak, Maurice. *Where the Wild Things Are.* Sendak has written and wonderfully illustrated a tale in which a boy uses his imagination to face frustration and fear.

Shah, Idries. *World Tales.* This book shows "the extraordinary coincidence of stories in all times, in all places."

Shulevitz, Uri. *The Treasure.* This is an old tale told by many storytellers from many different places. In this tale a man discovers that the treasure he seeks is not "out there" somewhere but nearer to him than he ever imagined.

Silverstein, Shel. *The Giving Tree.* This classic children's story is a tender parable about the gift of giving and friendship.

Skofield, James. *All Wet.* This is a book without words that portrays how nature might be seen by a small boy on a rainy day.

Spier, Peter. *People.* This is a simple and beautiful book that expresses the complicated idea that differences between people engender abundant riches for us all.

Seuss, Dr. *The Lorax.* This is a classic and well-loved fable about the importance of preserving the environment.

Timpanelli, Gioi. *Tales from the Roof of the World.* This book contains four Tibetan folktales that are filled with humor, drama, and magic.

BOOKS FOR OLDER PRIMARY GRADES AND YOUNG ADOLESCENTS

Beach, Milo Cleveland. *The Adventures of Rama.* This is a brief retelling of the *Ramayana* that younger children might also enjoy.

Bunting, Eve. *The Empty Window.* In this book a boy conquers his fears and uncertainties by doing something for his dying friend.

George, Jean Craighead. *Julie of the Wolves.* While a lost Eskimo girl is protected by wolves, she gains appreciation for her heritage and a sense of her oneness with nature.

Kittredge, Elaine, and Cyd Riley. *Twelve.* This book furnishes a loving reminder of the creativity and wonder inside each of us. In this sensitively written story, a boy named Jimmy grows aware of the reality of the physical and the spiritual worlds.

L'Engle, Madeline. *A Wrinkle in Time.* A timeless classic and a mystical, magical novel about mystery, concealed realms of the universe, and family closeness.

Lewis, C. S. *The Lion, the Witch and the Wardrobe.* This is the first of the *Chronicles of Narnia* series, a classic series of fantasy, imagination, and science fiction. In this allegorical story, four children enter a frozen world and participate in a battle between good and evil.

Madhur, Jaffrey. *Seasons of Splendor.* This book contains Hindu tales associated with the festivals of the year. Interestingly, they are introduced by personal reminiscences from Madhur's childhood in India.

Millman, Dan, and T. Taylor Bruce. *The Secret of the Peaceful Warrior.* This is an inspirational story in which an older boy discovers how to conquer fear by facing it rather than by running from it.

Moses, Jeffrey. *Oneness: Great Principles Shared by All Religions.* Using quotations from the world's great spiritual traditions, Moses shows how so many of our religious traditions have common teachings about many subjects and principles.

Peck, M. Scott. *The Friendly Snowflake.* This is a touching fable about a young girl's voyage into spirituality. Jenny and her brother explore the natural cycle of a single snowflake.

Rosman, Steven. *The Twenty-Two Gates to the Garden.* This is a collection of twenty-two tales that are grounded in ancient mystical wisdom and seek to help children sustain their innate sense of wonder, discover for themselves some of the great insights of mystical tradition, and encourage them to live lives filled with marvel, surprise, and spirituality.

Saint-Exupery, Antoine de. *The Little Prince.* A mystical tale about a young visitor from another planet.

Schram, Peninnah. *Jewish Stories One Generation Tells Another.* Perhaps the greatest Jewish storyteller of this generation, Schram has assembled and retold sixty-four timeless tales that abound with humor, wisdom, hope, obstacles to overcome, and the triumph of the spirit. It was her hope in writing this book that these tales would serve as a link between generations.

Schwartz, Howard. *Elijah's Violin & Other Jewish Fairy Tales.* Here are thirty-six Jewish fairy tales retold by one of the master Jewish folklorists of our time. Schwartz has included tales of fantasy and wonder from Morocco, Spain, India, Eastern Europe, Babylon, Egypt, and many more locations. These are tales that enchant and stretch the imagination.

Tolkien, J. R. R. His classics include *The Hobbit* and *The Lord of the Rings Trilogy.* These are timeless tales of fantasy, mysticism, magic, and adventure. *The Hobbit* introduces the series.

Periodicals

Brain/Mind Bulletin, P.O. Box 42211, 4717 N. Figueroa Street, Los Angeles, CA 90042.

Childswork/Childsplay, Center for Applied Psychology, 441 N. Fifth Street., Philadelphia, PA 19123.

Holistic Education Review, Holistic Education Press, P.O. Box 1476, Greenfield, MA 01302.

Journal of Humanistic and Transpersonal Education, P.O. Box 575, Amherst, MA 01002.

Journal of Humanistic Psychology, 325 Ninth Street, San Francisco, CA 94103.

Journal of Transpersonal Psychology, P.O. Box 4437, Stanford, CA 94305.

The Joyful Child Journal, P.O. Box 5506, Scottsdale, AZ 85261.

New Age Journal, 342 Western Avenue, Brighton, MA 02135–1095.

New Games Newsletter, Box 7901, San Francisco, CA 94120.

On the Beam, New Horizons for Learning, P.O. Box 51140, Seattle, WA 98115.

Positive Books for 21st Century Kids! (A Family Resource for Great Books, Music & Videos by Mail), Aton International, Inc., 7654 Benassi Drive, Gilroy, CA 95020.

The Quest, Theosophical Society in America, P.O. Box 270, Wheaton, IL 60189–0270.

Tufts University Diet & Nutrition Letter, P.O. Box 57857, Boulder, CO 80322–7857.

University of California, Berkeley Wellness Letter, P.O. Box 10922, Des Moines, IA 50340.

Yoga Journal, P.O. Box 3755, Escondido, CA 92033.